To access online media visit:
www.halleonard.com/mylibrary

8836-9966-3102-1223

GETTING STARTED WITH MUSIC PRODUCTION

Hal Leonard Recording Method

GETTING STARTED WITH MUSIC PRODUCTION

Robert Willey

Hal Leonard Books
An Imprint of Hal Leonard Corporation

Published in 2015 by Hal Leonard Books
An Imprint of Hal Leonard Corporation
7777 West Bluemound Road
Milwaukee, WI 53213

Trade Book Division Editorial Offices
33 Plymouth St., Montclair, NJ 07042

Grateful acknowledgment is made to the following for permission to reprint the following images, which appear courtesy of their respective owners:

PreSonus Audio Electronics, Inc.: p. 2 (top and bottom) and p. 3 (top). Hosa Technology, Inc.: p. 3 (bottom). Alesis: p. 6 (top). Cambridge Audio: p. 6 (center). Acousticom Corporation: p. 6 (bottom). Shure Incorporated: pp. 8 and 13 (bottom right). On-Stage Stands: p. 13 (bottom left). RØDE Microphones: p. 14 (top). Event Electronics: p. 92 (photo of Event 2030 loudspeaker).

All other images in this book were created by the author.

Printed in the United States of America
Book design by Kristina Rolander

Library of Congress Cataloging-in-Publication Data

Willey, Robert.
Getting started with music production / Robert Willey.
    pages cm. – (Hal Leonard recording method)
Includes bibliographical references and index.
ISBN 978-1-4803-9379-0
1. Studio One (Computer file) 2. Digital audio editors. 3. Popular music–Production and direction. I. Title.
ML74.4.S79W55 2015
781.3'4536--dc23
                        2015006986

www.halleonardbooks.com

"Participation—
that's what's gonna save the human race."

—PETE SEEGER (1919–2014)

CONTENTS

ACKNOWLEDGMENTS

Thanks to . . .

The composers and performers: Sam Broussard, Alfredo Cardim, Caleb Elliott, Adam Ezra, Jeff Fletcher, the J&B Project (Björn Grashorn and Jan Drapala), Louretta, Magda, Scott Eric Olivier, Ryan Ordway, Phat Hat, and Mark Summerell. Many, many thanks for letting us work with your music. Please explore these artists' websites and purchase their music.

The engineers: Neil Citron, Tony Daigle, Tim Leitner, Rick Naqvi, Alberto Netto, and Ken Scott did fine work to produce the multitracks included with the supplemental media for the book. Consider their services for your next project.

John Mlynczak, Education Market Manager at PreSonus Audio Electronics. Talking with him crystallized the idea for this book and got the ball rolling with Bill Gibson, my excellent developmental editor at Hal Leonard. Follow John for information on how to use technology to teach music in the schools, and look for Bill's many books on music production. Jessica Burr and Josh Wimmer were instrumental in moving the manuscript through the final stages.

Mark Rubel at the Blackbird Academy for suggesting "Easy Street" and hooking me up with Ryan and Ken, and Kevin Becka for working out the details.

Jiro "Jireaux" Hatano, to whom I always turn for tips on what's going on in Acadiana. He knocked it out of the park with his recommendations of Caleb Elliott and Sam Broussard.

Ed Golterman (Golterman Historics/Heartsong), who gave me permission to use his father's recording of Bainbridge Colby, and the reference specialists in the Digital Reference Section of the Library of Congress, who guided me through their "American Leaders Speak" collection and its policies.

The operators of freesound.org, a huge collaborative database of audio samples released under Creative Commons licenses. Audio Example 5-1 consists of two from the library, contributed by Xavier Serra (flute) and Tim Kahn (Toriana accordion).

Alana Mulford, Adam Ezra's manager.

Rachel Klein and Steve Oppenheimer at PreSonus. Arnd Kaiser at PreSonus Software.

Scott Emerton and Mathew Piccolotto at RØDE Microphones/Event Electronics. Thanks to RØDE for allowing us to include samples from their Soundbooth app in Audio Examples 5-12 and 5-13.

John Born and Davida Rochman at Shure Incorporated.

Jeff Seitz recorded the piano on "Sleepless Nights," and Anisul Islam Khan created the animation of the sine wave.

And above all, to Maria Oneide Willey and my two children, who put up with me working all the time.

INTRODUCTION

WHOM THIS BOOK IS FOR

Welcome to *Getting Started with Music Production*, the book designed to get you started recording and mixing music with a digital audio workstation (DAW) as quickly as possible. This is an activity-based program, so while the basic theory behind the tools will be presented to help you understand what is going on, you'll be given plenty of opportunities to try your hand—and ears—at the operations described here. The book is intended for beginners, but may fill in gaps in your understanding even if you've been recording for some time, and the full recording sessions in a variety of styles that are included can be used by anyone to hone their mixing skills.

WHAT YOU WILL LEARN

As a result of reading this book and doing the exercises within, you should:

- Be able to record, edit, and mix music using a digital audio workstation.
- Know the meaning of key audio terms.
- Understand basic audio principles.

HOW TO USE THIS BOOK

I suggest that you read the first six chapters in order and then pick one or more of the mix sessions in Chapters 7–10 before reading the last two chapters. The chapters with Mix Sessions will allow you to put all the pieces together, so you may want to hold off on those until you have covered the basics. You should at least read Chapters 1, 2, and 5 before you start the Mix Sessions, because they are open-ended and leave most of the decisions about what you want to try up to you. Chapter 3 offers you a chance to apply the information presented in Chapter 2 about volume by working with a song recorded by Ken Scott, one of the five engineers to have worked with the Beatles. Some of the projects involve large multitrack session files that you may wish to download in advance, so that the material will be ready when you need it. Stereo MP3 mixes are provided so that you can decide which piece of music you would like to start with first. Information on the supplementary media is included in Appendix A.

The practice exercises sprinkled throughout the theory sections are optional, but give you a chance to apply the concepts as they are introduced, so that you'll be better prepared for the activities at the end of each chapter. You will find step-by-step instructions for them linked from the same online index used for the audio and video examples in the text. The ideal setup would be to display them on a second monitor while you have Studio One on your primary screen, so that you can follow along with the instructions while trying out the software. The activities that are labeled Basic give you the opportunity to use prerecorded material in case you don't have a microphone or anyone around to record. The Intermediate exercises are more challenging. You'll need a microphone and a little more time to do them. The Advanced activities are just jumping-off points for the more ambitious explorers. You're welcome to post links to what you come up with in response to those on the book's companion website, found at lovelythinking.com.

Markers have been placed in the text to indicate when it is appropriate to answer the quiz questions, which are gathered at the end of each chapter. Reread the relevant sections in the book if you don't know the answers before skipping to Appendix C to check your work. If you're still mystified, look over the corresponding sections in the *Studio One Reference Manual*.

Keyboard shortcuts are collected near the end of each chapter, just before the quiz questions. Windows and Apple computers use different modifying keys for shortcuts. When you see a shortcut that includes text like "Alt/Opt," with two modifying keys separated by a slash, it means that the modifying key depends on which type of computer you are using. Use the first one (in this case the Alt key) if you're on a Windows computer, and the second one (in this example the Opt key) if you're using an Apple.

The Appendices in the back of the book include information on the supplemental material and other online resources, an explanation of how to install Studio One, a glossary of terms, a bibliography, and answers to the quiz questions. The book's companion website features interviews with the songwriters and engineers who produced the songs, links to their websites, topics from each chapter, a teachers' guide, and a discussion area where you can also ask questions and make suggestions.

Studio One has a number of useful resources that can be accessed under the Help menu option while running the software. First is the *Studio One Reference Manual*. You'll also find a list of keyboard shortcuts for your operating system, an easy way to get to the Settings folder, a connection to PreSonus's website, and the option to check for updates. You also have the option to type a term into the search field.

WHY STUDIO ONE?

The emphasis in this book is on trying out the techniques described and hearing how things sound when you operate the controls. It's like learning to fly a plane: You study the theory in a class, but then you need to get in the cockpit and take off. I want to get you up in the air as soon as possible. All the demonstrations and exercises in the book were designed to be done with Studio One software. PreSonus offers two ways to get the software for free. You can download a trial version of Studio One Professional that times out after a month, or get Studio One Free, which has fewer features but does not time out. The Studio One Artist version is an excellent match for the book and comes bundled with many PreSonus products. Most of the exercises in the book can be done with Studio One Free. See Appendix B for instructions on how to install the software. One of the advantages of using Studio One is that is cross-platform and runs on both Windows and Apple computers, which will allow more people to explore the techniques shared in the book with the same piece of software, and to begin to record and mix music as soon as possible.

Studio One's modern, elegant design and streamlined workflow allow musicians and songwriters to capture their musical ideas before their inspiration slips away, making it a good match for the approach taken in this book. The program's lead developers, Wolfgang Kundrus and Matthias Juwan, had worked at Steinberg (Cubase, Nuendo) and wanted to start over writing fresh new code that would run more efficiently on the new CPUs used with today's computers. As a result, the software is very stable and allows you to keep multiple songs open simultaneously. You won't have to deal with extra technical issues, and its one-window configuration and drag-and-drop functionality will make it easier to stay right-brain-focused while capturing your creative impulses.

Studio One is a good choice for a DAW for this book because it frees you up to study the principles of production without a lot of extra fuss. The step-by-step instructions for the exercises will help you explore the techniques presented without having to invest a lot of time in learning the software. You may decide to continue using it because of its excellent sound quality and for the additional features included in the Professional version, such as integrated pitch correction, video support, mastering tools, and online sales.

The understanding that you develop as a result of working through this book can be applied to any other recording program, such as Pro Tools or Logic. These programs all operate in the digital audio domain and provide the same basic functions. Each piece of software has a couple of features that make it easier to do certain things, so after you become skilled at one, you might try learning others, in order to have a choice of tools, and to be able to function in different environments.

Learning to record and mix is like learning an instrument or any other skill. The more frequently you sit down and focus on specific aspects, the quicker you'll develop the skills to produce music without having to stop and think about how the system works. I hope this book will help get you up and running as smoothly as possible, and that you have many happy hours making music the way you think it should sound.

CHAPTER 1

INPUT

GOAL AND OBJECTIVES

After working through this chapter you should be able to record and play back audio using your software, interface, and computer.

+ Route audio signals into and out of the computer via the audio interface.

+ Select the appropriate mic type and design for a specific application.

+ Set the proper input level on your preamp in order to record a signal with a strong level.

+ Choose a good location for a microphone relative to the sound source.

PREREQUISITES

You may work through the chapters using the supplied prerecorded material. To record your own material, you will need:

+ An audio interface to convert microphone and instrument signals to and from digital format.

+ An installed and authorized copy of Studio One. See Appendix B for help.

+ A microphone or electric guitar or bass.

THEORY AND PRACTICE

One of the most important things for an engineer to understand is signal flow—the path that audio signals take as they pass through wires, computers, amplifiers, and loudspeakers. Developing some understanding of what an audio interface does will prepare you to use microphones and other sound sources more effectively.

Audio Interface Signal Flow

The first piece of equipment that we will look at is the audio interface—the device that is used to get sound into and out of a computer. Figure 1-1 shows an example of the front of an audio interface. A single combo plug accepts both microphone and instrument cables. Figure 1-2 shows the connectors on the back for MIDI devices, loudspeakers, and headphones.

Figure 1-1. Front panel of a PreSonus AudioBox USB audio interface. Its bigger sisters like the 44SL and 1818VSL have additional inputs for line level devices.

Figure 1-2. The AudioBox's back panel.

Audio interfaces are used to convert an analog signal into digital data that can then be passed back and forth to the computer using a single USB or FireWire cable. Once the signal is inside the computer, it can be recorded, edited, manipulated, and mixed, after which it can be sent back through the audio interface to be played through loudspeakers and headphones (Figure 1-3).

The number of channels on your interface determines only how many inputs can be recorded together at a time, not the number of tracks you can have at the end of a project. For example, if you have a two-channel interface, you can record a guitarist and bass player on the first pass, rewind, and add a second guitar part and lead vocal, and then back up once more to record a background vocal part.

You can work through the exercises in this book even if you don't have an external audio interface. Just select your computer's audio system and plug into the built-in headphone jack. Some computers have soundcards connected to their audio jacks that you can plug devices into. Having a dedicated external audio interface will allow you to make higher-quality recordings and hook up a variety of microphones, loudspeakers, and headphones, but many of the exercises in the book have prerecorded tracks you can work with in case you don't have the extra hardware. See Appendix B for help with installing and configuring the Studio One software.

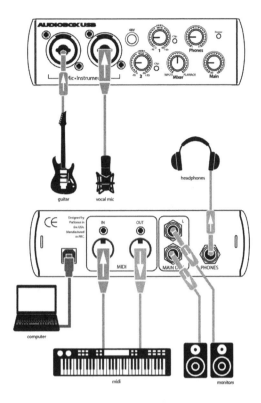

Figure 1-3. Analog devices such as microphones, instruments, loudspeakers, and headphones are connected to the audio interface.

We will next look in some detail at the four basic types of inputs that can be connected to audio interfaces:

1. Microphones
2. Electric instruments with pickups
3. Line level electronic devices
4. Devices with digital outputs

Microphone Inputs

If you have a microphone and audio interface, try connecting them together now using a microphone cable. Microphone cables usually terminate with XLR connectors (Figure 1-4). If you don't have an external audio interface, you may need an adaptor to plug into your computer's audio input jack, or you may use your computer's built-in microphone.

Figure 1-4. The circular 3-pin connector of an XLR microphone cable.

ɛ

̇nones output a weak *microphone level* analog electrical signal that needs to be boosted with ̇ifier and then converted to a digital signal inside the audio interface so it can be processed ̇puter program. The preamplifier knob on the audio interface needs to be adjusted during the recoȧȧıg process to achieve the proper level. Some manufacturers include a pad button to reduce the input level, for cases when you are recording something very loud that overloads your input and clips even when the preamplifier is turned all the way down. Normally, the button is left in its out position.

If you see a phantom power button, you might think it used when making spooky music. Some audio interfaces label this function "+48V" instead, which tells you what the button actually does. This button should be pressed only when you are using a condenser microphone or certain ribbon mics that specifically require it, the reason for which we will explain shortly. Phantom power can ruin a ribbon mic not designed to receive it, so be careful. You do not need it on if you are using a dynamic microphone.

One of the critical elements in getting a good recording from a microphone is setting a good level on the audio interface's preamplifier, so that your recording is neither too soft nor too loud. This process is demonstrated in Video Example 1-1.

VIDEO EXAMPLE 1-1. How to set a good recording level for a microphone track.

EXERCISE 1-1: *Record yourself speaking through a microphone with a good level.*

Electric Instruments with Pickups

Electric instruments have physical elements like strings whose vibrations are sensed within the magnetic field of a pickup. The output of an electric guitar or bass is usually plugged into an amplifier that drives a loudspeaker, creating a pressure wave that we listen to. In the recording studio, an electric guitar amplifier is often recorded by placing a microphone such as a Shure SM57 in front of the loudspeaker.

Another way to record an electric instrument is to connect its output directly to an audio interface with a quarter-inch tip-sleeve cable (Figure 1-5). The signal is coming directly from the instrument's pickups, so it is very dry and clear and may sound unnatural to a guitarist who is used to hearing the effect a guitar amp has on tone. Companies have written software plug-ins to modify the sound to simulate different amplifier settings and types of cabinets, allowing an engineer to experiment with a wide range of sounds (Video Example 1-2).

Figure 1-5. A quarter-inch connector.

VIDEO EXAMPLE 1-2. How to record an electric instrument without using an amp.

EXERCISE 1-2: *Record an electric instrument plugged directly into an audio interface.*

If your audio interface doesn't have an electric instrument input, you can plug it into a DI box with two outputs—a quarter-inch jack that can be connected to a guitar amp as usual, and a microphone jack that lets you plug into a microphone input on the audio interface (Figure 1-6). This has two benefits: First, the player can operate their amplifier as normal and get the natural sound they are used to from the speaker; and second, a microphone cable can run longer distances to the audio interface than a quarter-inch cable without the sound becoming degraded. If you have enough tracks on your interface, you may wish record both the amp with a microphone and the direct signal coming through the microphone cable from the DI box, so that you can experiment later with blending the two tracks together, or replace the guitar amplifier sound with the direct sound processed by a plug-in.

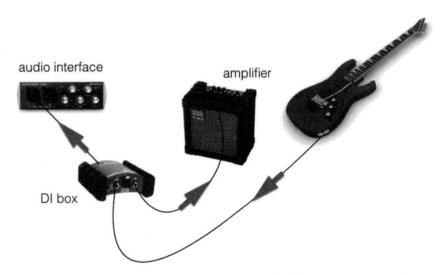

audio interface

amplifier

DI box

Figure 1-6. A DI (direct injection) box splits the input signal into two outputs, one for an amp and the other for recording.

Line Level Electronic Devices

Electronic instruments don't have the physically vibrating bodies of electric instruments. Their output is at *line level*, rather than microphone or electric instrument level. Line level signals come out of electronic keyboards, synthesizer modules, drum machines, radios, and CD and DVD players. These signals are stronger than microphone level, but still not strong enough to power headphones or loudspeakers. Driving the vibrating elements in those devices requires additional amplification of the signal. The main outputs of an audio interface are also line level. You will need an amplifier to boost the level to the point at which it can drive speakers—either a stand-alone amplifier like a home stereo system or one built in to a powered monitor.

Most line level devices are stereo, so you will need two cables—one for the left audio channel and the other for the right. Some line level devices use quarter-inch connectors (Figure 1-7); others use RCA jacks developed by the Radio Corporation of America, which have a red connector for the right channel and a white one for the left (Figure 1-8).

Figure 1-7. An Alesis SamplePad with quarter-inch output jacks.

Figure 1-8. A Cambridge Audio CD player with RCA outputs.

EXERCISE 1-3: *Check any line level audio devices you have to see whether they offer quarter-inch or RCA output connections.*

Figure 1-9. Quarter-inch TRS connector used to make a balanced connection.

Each model of audio interface has different input capabilities. Some quarter-inch inputs are for high-impedance electric instruments, while others are for line level sources. If you have a line level device and your audio interface has line level inputs, you can connect them directly. Some devices use tip-ring-sleeve connectors (Figure 1-9) rather than tip-sleeve (Figure 1-5). Check the documentation for the output of your line level sources and the inputs of your audio interface to see what is recommended. If you don't have a line level input on your interface, you can plug into a DI box and then connect the output of the DI box to the mic input on your audio interface using an XLR cable.

VIDEO EXAMPLE 1-3. Recording line level input.

EXERCISE 1-4: *Record the output from a line level device.*

Digital Connections

The three types of inputs discussed so far were all connecting the output from analog devices to the input of the audio interface, which takes care of the conversion to the digital binary format used by the computer. For convenience and fidelity, some models of audio interfaces also include a fourth type of input, ports that make it possible to pass the digital signals that don't need conversion to the computer. There are two types of digital inputs: MIDI and digital audio. MIDI data is a control signal, not an audio signal, so it doesn't technically doesn't belong in an audio interface. It is used to communicate messages such as which key has been pressed and how hard, and the changes in position of wheels and foot pedals. Some newer keyboards have their own USB ports that allow them to be connected directly to the computer, instead of going through a MIDI interface. For more information on MIDI, consult this book's companion website.

Digital keyboards synthesize sound as a list of binary numbers. In most keyboards, these samples are converted to analog form before being passed out the analog audio outputs of the device. The analog signal then travels through a quarter-inch cable that is plugged into the audio interface's analog line inputs. The analog signal has to then be converted back into a digital signal before the computer can work on it. Some newer keyboards offer both analog and digital audio outputs (Figure 1-10). Taking the digital output from the keyboard and going into a digital input on the audio interface or computer keeps the signal in the digital domain. Check your system to see if you are able to take advantage of this feature.

Figure 1-10. The Yamaha Motif keyboard has connections for digital audio output, MIDI, Ethernet, and USB.

EXERCISE 1-5: *List the audio inputs on your interface and the devices that could be plugged into them.*

Now that you've seen the options for inputs on your audio interface, it's time to inventory the outputs. Some interfaces have audio output connections for both loudspeakers and headphones and may offer a separate volume control for each. It is helpful to have both types of playback systems. Wearing headphones while recording keeps the sounds you're listening to from being picked up by the microphones. And when you're ready to play back what you've done, you may wish to switch to loudspeakers, to hear how it sounds played in a room.

EXERCISE 1-6: *List the audio outputs on your interface and the devices that could be connected to them.*

EXERCISE 1-7: *Make test recordings from any devices you can plug in to your interface. Play them back on systems connected to the audio interface's outputs.*

Answer quiz questions 1.1–1.7, found at end of the chapter.

TYPES OF MICROPHONES

The choice of microphones has quite a bit to do with the way things sound in recordings. We will talk here about how they are constructed, and come back in Chapter 5 to learn more about their tonal characteristics.

Impedance

The *impedance* of a circuit or device is measured in ohms and refers to how much resistance it creates to electricity. The output impedances of microphones are typically categorized as being in one of three ranges: low (0–600 ohms), medium (600–10,000 ohms), or high (10,000 ohms and above). The output impedance of the microphone you use should be lower than the input impedance of your audio interface for the electricity to flow efficiently. For example, a Shure SM57 microphone with an output impedance of 300 ohms should combine well with a PreSonus AudioBox that has an input impedance of 1,200 ohms. Check the documentation for your microphone and interface to see if they make a good match.

Dynamic Microphones

A *dynamic* microphone has a moving diaphragm that vibrates in response to a pressure wave carrying sound. The diaphragm causes a voice coil to move through a magnetic field, thereby inducing a change in voltage. Dynamic microphones are generally reasonably priced, rugged, and can handle very high sound pressure. The Shure SM57 microphone (Figure 1-11) is a dynamic microphone often used to record snare drums and guitar amplifiers.

Figure 1-11. The Shure SM57 microphone.

However, the mass of the voice coil in a dynamic microphone limits its ability to respond to the fast, delicate vibrations that give clarity to the sound of instruments like the acoustic guitar. The metal diaphragms in *condenser* microphones are extremely light, allowing them to respond more easily in response to the guitar's weak, high-frequency vibrations.

Microphone Input Controls

The diaphragm in a condenser microphone needs to be electrically charged. The energy for this can come from a battery in the microphone, but more often it is sent from the audio interface through the microphone cable. This method is called *phantom power*, and the +48V button on the audio interface that turns it on must be pressed when using a condenser mic or it will not send any signal (Figure 1-12). You should always turn phantom power off when you don't need it, since dynamic microphones don't need it and some ribbon mics will be damaged by it. Some manufacturers suggest turning phantom power on only after a microphone has been connected and off again before disconnecting it.

Figure 1-12.
Phantom power is sent from the audio interface through the microphone cable to a condenser microphone when the +48V button is depressed.

Answer quiz questions 1.8–1.17.

Other Controls

Your audio interface may have a mix knob that controls the balance between what you are playing into the audio interface and what the computer is sending back. Turning the input knob all the way to the input side allows you to hear what you're playing. Remember to turn it back to the middle so you can hear playback when you are done. The delay time (*latency*) between what you are playing and what the computer sends back when you are recording tracks can be changed by getting into the Audio Setup menu and lowering the Device Block Size. You can decrease the *buffer size* while you're recording, and then raise it back when you're done and ready to mix if you notice clicks or pops, use a lot of tracks, or apply many computationally heavy audio processes like reverbs and delays. Once you've finished recording, you can increase the buffer size to make it easier for the computer to perform lots of processing. The short delay created by the larger buffer won't bother you then, since you won't be trying to record while playing back.

Microphone Placement

We have already looked at the differences in types of construction between dynamic and condenser microphones and will see in Chapter 5 the effect they have on tone. Another important quality of microphones is how well they pick up sound coming from different directions.

Pickup Patterns: Omnidirectional and Cardioid

Microphones designed to respond equally well to sound coming from all directions are called *omnidirectional*. Omnidirectional microphones are good for recording a group of instruments together, or for capturing the overall sound from a sound source with a complex radiation pattern, like a piano that sounds different over the surface of its soundboard.

Microphones that pick up better from the front than the sides and back are called *directional* (also often referred to as *cardioid*) microphones. These microphones are the best choice when you want to pick up one instrument out of a group, or to reduce the amplified sound of a singer circulating from a loudspeaker back into the microphone, which can cause screeching feedback.

Using directional microphones close to each instrument allows the engineer to isolate each instrument on a separate track. This is not possible when using omnidirectional microphones. There won't be much separation between two omnidirectional microphones set up to capture the performance of a singing guitarist, even when one microphone is set up near the singer's mouth (Audio Example 1-1) and the other near their guitar (Audio Example 1-2). Notice how much guitar was picked up by the vocal mic, and that there is a lot of vocal on the guitar track.

AUDIO EXAMPLE 1-1. Omnidirectional microphone on the singer picks up some of the guitar.

AUDIO EXAMPLE 1-2. Omnidirectional microphone on the guitar picks up some of the voice.

Using two directional microphones instead of omnis would improve the separation of the sound sources. Compare the omni recordings in Audio Examples 1-1 and 1-2 with the recordings made with two mics with cardioid pickup patterns in Audio Examples 1-3 and 1-4.

AUDIO EXAMPLE 1-3. Vocal part recorded with a cardioid mic.

AUDIO EXAMPLE 1-4. Guitar part recorded with a cardioid mic.

Answer quiz questions 1.18 and 1.19.

Location

Your effectiveness as an engineer will improve as you become more aware of how things sound. You may never have paid much attention to room acoustics. Start by exploring the acoustics of the space where you are planning to record.

EXERCISE 1-8: *Walk around and clap to test the acoustics of the space you're in. Notice how the sound changes depending on whether you are in the center of the room, close to a wall, or in the corner. Try out different rooms and see if you can find one with echoes or significant changes in tone.*

An instrument will sound different depending on where it is located in a room. Musicians may change their performance depending on whom they are sitting next to, and how close they are to each other. It's also important that they can see as well as hear each other. Try to avoid placing instruments too close to walls or under a low ceiling, since the reflecting surfaces will be closer to the microphone. The shorter the path of the reflected sound, the louder it will be and more likely it will be to affect the tone when it is combined with the unreflected sound coming directly from the instrument. Corners of rooms are especially bad, since they provide an environment for the boominess in the bass frequencies to build up. Raising an amp off the ground or placing a rug under it helps reduce reflections off the floor. Consider putting absorbing materials on the walls, floors, and ceilings to tame the amount of reflection of sound waves off hard surfaces. We will return to the subject of room acoustics in Chapter 11.

Perhaps the most important decision in using a microphone is where to put it in relation to the sound source. Start by having the musician play the part you will be recording. Walk around and listen to what it sounds like from different positions. If you're going to record with an omni microphone, plug one ear so that you can focus on what the microphone would pick up in that location. If you're going to record with a cardioid microphone, plug one ear and cup the open ear with your hand, to make it more sensitive to sounds coming from one direction. Which sounds better—with your ear cupped or not? This can help you decide whether to use a cardioid or an omni mic, should you have a choice.

You will achieve better results if you're willing to make the effort to experiment with mic placement and pay attention to how it affects the sound. The process can be made more efficient by wearing closed headphones while setting up a mic so that you can hear the changes in sound the microphone is picking up as you move it around. Many engineers prefer to set up microphones in the studio and then retreat to the *control room*, an acoustically separated room containing the recording equipment and speakers, where they adjust the tone using equalizers, saving themselves the time and effort required to walk back and forth to move microphones around. They may want to get on with recording as quickly as possible, thinking that they can create the desired final sound later when they get to the mixing stage. Other engineers believe it is worth taking the time to capture the best tones possible, so that they get the sounds they want from the beginning, instead of relying on being able to fix things later. In the end, this saves time and can result in a better product.

Whatever your approach, be careful that you don't tire out the musicians with lengthy adjustments. The more quickly you get to tracking, the more excitement and energy they will likely have to deliver an inspired performance. It may be better to set aside time just for setting up the instruments, especially the drums. After finding the right microphone positions, recording levels, and headphone settings, you can take a break before starting to record.

Distance

After you decide where in a room an instrument sounds best and which microphone in your collection best captures it, the two main decisions become how far away to set the microphone from the sound source and where to aim it. The distance between the microphone and the source of vibrations is critical, since the intensity of the sound drops off quickly as you move away from it. Doubling the distance between a microphone and the sound source doesn't cut the intensity in half, but rather by about 75 percent.

The sound that travels straight from the sound source to the microphone is called the *direct sound*. The sound that bounces off the floor, ceiling, and walls is called the *indirect sound*. The amount of delay between the arrival of the direct and delayed versions of the sound combined with the proportion between the amplitude of the two provides the information to the listener's brain necessary to judge how far they are from the sound source, and how big the space they are in is. The closer you put the microphone to the sound source, the less effect the room acoustics will have on the recording, since the direct sound becomes so much louder than the indirect sound. The effect of the room becomes negligible when you put a microphone just a few inches from a sound source; whereas if you move it a couple of yards away, it will become quite pronounced. Most studio recordings are made with the microphones close to the sound source, to get the clearest sound possible. Synthetic reverberation can be added to give the recording any desired sense of space.

You can turn up the preamplifier level to compensate for the drop in level caused by moving the microphone away. While this does maintain the volume being recorded from the sound source, it also amplifies the reflected sounds coming off the floor, walls, and ceiling, thereby increasing the relative importance of the acoustics of the room. The following series of recordings of a piano onstage in an auditorium shows how the distance between the microphone and the source affects the balance between direct and indirect sound.

AUDIO EXAMPLE 1-5. One foot away.

AUDIO EXAMPLE 1-6. Four feet away.

AUDIO EXAMPLE 1-7. Ten feet away.

AUDIO EXAMPLE 1-8. First row.

AUDIO EXAMPLE 1-9. Third row.

AUDIO EXAMPLE 1-10. Middle row.

AUDIO EXAMPLE 1-11. Back row.

Answer quiz questions 1.20 and 1.21.

The Proximity Effect

Directional microphones placed only a few inches from the sound source are subject to a boost of bass frequencies known as the *proximity effect*. Some singers and radio personalities with low-pitched voices find this change of tone pleasing. In other situations, it may be undesirable, so some designers of cardioid microphones include a switch to cut some of the bass frequencies, to compensate for the boost that happens when their mics are set up close to the source. Some engineers prefer to record without the bass roll-off switch engaged and to modify the tone only after the fact with the recording software. Listen again to Audio Example 1-4, which was recorded with the roll-off switch on, and compare it with Audio Example 1-12, in which the roll-off switch was off.

AUDIO EXAMPLE 1-4. Recording with the roll-off switch on can compensate for the proximity effect.

AUDIO EXAMPLE 1-12. The proximity effect can cause some boominess.

EXERCISE 1-9: *Record yourself at different distances with a cardioid microphone. Can you detect changes in tone caused by the proximity effect?*

Answer quiz question 1.22.

Windscreen and Pop Filters

Microphones are designed to respond to changes in air pressure, not air speed. If you want to test whether a microphone is working, talk or snap your fingers in front of it. One way to identify people who have not read this book, and therefore do not know any better, is if you see them checking a mic by alternating between blowing and talking into it: "*Hooo, hooo, hooo*—is this thing working?" Shorter bursts of air may also happen unintentionally when a singer is up close to a microphone and says words that contain hard consonants like *p, b, d,* and *t* that are created by building up and then releasing air pressure in the mouth.

EXERCISE 1-10: *Put your hand close to your mouth and say "please," emphasizing the initial* p *at the start of the word. Do you feel the burst of air?*

Figure 1-13 shows what the waveform of a recording of the word "please" looks like. Notice the burst of noise you hear at the beginning of the word, caused by the first consonant.

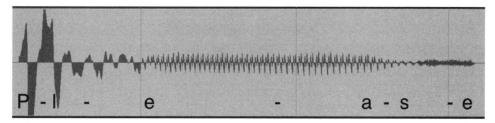

Figure 1-13. Diagram of the waveform of the word "please."

VIDEO EXAMPLE 1-4. Playback of the distorted recording of the word "please."

The distortion resulting from wind is not the only problem a vocalist may cause while recording, potentially damaging a microphone. The closer the singer gets to the microphone, the more spit and humidity it will be exposed to. Fortunately, there are a variety of materials that will block the wind and moisture while letting the pressure wave pass. For onstage singing and outdoor wind, a windscreen is the most popular choice—a piece of foam with a hole in one end that is slid over the microphone (Figure 1-14).

Some dynamic microphones have built-in windscreens (Figure 1-15).

Figure 1-14. A windscreen is designed to be slipped over the end of a microphone.

Figure 1-15. The Shure SM58 has a windscreen built into its capsule.

A pop filter can also be used to protect vocal mics from wind and humidity. It is a shield made of cloth or metal, and is positioned a few inches in front of the microphone (Figure 1-16). Pop filters are more delicate than windscreens, which makes them better suited to studio work than live performance.

Figure 1-16. RØDE's kit for the NT1 microphone consists of a pop filter and a shock mount, which limits low frequencies passing from the mic stand to the mic.

EXERCISE 1-11: *Make your own pop filter using a coat hanger, nylon stocking, and clamp or tape.*

Answer quiz question 1.23.

Phase Cancellation

The last subtopic for this section on microphone position deals with the effects of mixing the signals from multiple microphones that are arranged so closely together that more than one of them pick up sound from the same sound source (Figure 1-17).

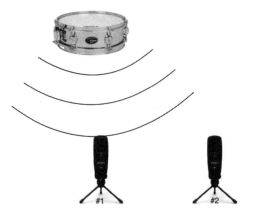

Figure 1-17. Two microphones picking up sound from the same instrument.

When microphones are set up this way, the sound of the instrument reaches microphone no. 2 a little later than microphone no. 1, since 2 is farther away. When the signals from the two microphones are mixed, an effect called *phase cancellation* will be created. This is what happens when two out-of-sync copies of the same waveform are mixed, leading to an unpleasant change of tone and fullness of the sound.

AUDIO EXAMPLE 1-13. Sound of a snare drum recorded with one microphone.

AUDIO EXAMPLE 1-14. Phase cancellation caused by combining signals from two microphones.

One way to reduce phase cancellation is to follow the 3:1 rule, which says that the two microphones that are picking up the same instrument should be at least three times as far apart from each other as the closest mic is to the sound source (Figure 1-18). In this case, the delayed sound that reaches the farther microphone will lose enough power that it won't interfere so noticeably with the wave picked up by the closer microphone.

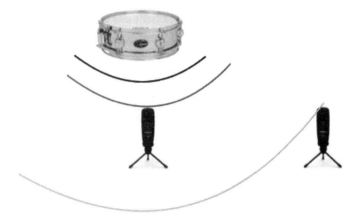

Figure 1-18. Mic setup obeying the 3:1 rule. The wave has lost a lot of energy by the time it reaches the mic on the right.

EXERCISE 1-12: *Vary the delay time between the two tracks in the phase-cancellation.song session.*

Answer quiz questions 1.24 and 1.25.

Data Storage

The sounds that are recorded and the settings the engineer adjusts in the DAW program have to be stored in memory to be available for later recall. A monophonic track of CD quality sounds takes about 10 megabytes of storage space. A stereo track requires twice that. It is recommended to store your recordings on a separate drive from the one the computer uses for its operating system.

As the number of your music productions grows, it will become increasingly important to have a system for naming files and organizing directories to store them. This will save you from wasting time and brainpower looking for a particular version of a project, and make it less likely that you will lose something you care about. A good system for working on the projects in this book would be to create a directory or folder called "Getting Started with MP" and subfolders in that folder for each chapter.

When you press the play button on your recording software, the operating system reads the samples for each track off the drive, and the CPU processes the sound and sends it to your audio interface, which turns it back into analog form so your audio equipment can play it.

When all this is going smoothly, everyone is happy and smiles abound over the excellent work the musicians and engineers have done. Unfortunately, every 3.1 seconds on average somewhere in the world, there is a glitch in someone's computer, causing the user to lose whatever work they haven't saved, followed by a cry of anguish. Do not let this happen to you! Save your work often, and be grateful that Studio One's programmers had the wisdom to set up an auto-save function designed to automatically save your work in a temporary file for you, mere moments before catastrophe strikes.

Studio One doesn't crash very often, but if it does, look in the History folder, open the latest song file, and then rename it to something like "recovered-version.song" before the operating system cycles around and writes over it with a new backup. You can also take advantage of these backup files to get back to the song the way you had it 30 minutes ago, before you messed it up. It's a good idea as you go along to occasionally save files under new names that indicate the progress you've made, so that you can go back to a previous version in the future if you later decide you preferred it. Or you may rather use Studio One's capability to save multiple versions of the same song in a single file.

Much worse, however, than an occasional file being lost is the failure of an entire storage system. While this happens only every 19.7 seconds or so, it can be truly catastrophic when your turn comes. To protect yourself from the misery of losing everything you have ever done on your computer (along with all of your pictures), it is important to develop a backup system. One of the best is to use the 3:2:1 approach—three copies of your data, on two different types of media (e.g., optical discs and magnetic or flash drives), with one of the copies off-site (at your office, in the cloud, etc.). That way, if one system fails or is lost due to theft or natural disaster, you will still have a backup.

You have been warned. Heed this advice!

REVIEW

Most personal computers offer some way to convert digital recordings to analog signals that can be output through a headphones jack or built-in speakers. Some have more sophisticated sound cards with connectors to plug in microphones or output to multiple loudspeakers. People who are interested in music production usually get an external audio interface to increase their options and the fidelity of the sounds being input and output. Such interfaces generally accept four types of inputs:

1. Low-impedance microphones using XLR plugs

2. High-impedance electric instruments (e.g., electric guitar) using quarter-inch plugs

3. Line level electronic instruments (e.g., synthesizers) using quarter-inch plugs

4. Inputs for digital audio (e.g., S/PDIF through RCA cables) or MIDI (5-pin DIN)

There's a lot you can do while studying this book even if you don't have an external audio interface. Your computer may have an input jack or built-in microphone. If not, you can use the song session files supplied in this book's supplemental media and get recordings off the Internet or from your handheld devices. Most computers have at least an output jack for headphones or speakers. Adapt the exercises and activities to the equipment you have available and to your musical tastes, experience, and interest. You will get a lot more out of this book if you try out the techniques along the way.

The two most common types of microphones are dynamics and condensers. A condenser microphone is the more delicate of the two. It is more expensive but gets a clearer sound. To work, it needs phantom power sent to it through the microphone cable from the audio interface. Don't turn on phantom power if you're using a ribbon mic, since that can cause damage unless the microphone is designed for it.

Microphones with a directional (cardioid) pickup pattern focus on sounds coming straight in from the front. Those that respond to sound equally well from all directions are called omnidirectional.

Care should be taken about where to place the microphone. Placing the microphone a few inches to a foot away will result in a clear sound that is not affected much by room acoustics. When recording close up with a cardioid microphone, you may want to compensate for the low-frequency boost caused by the proximity effect by rolling off some of its bass frequencies. When using multiple microphones, follow the 3:1 rule to avoid getting phase cancellation.

The weak microphone signal must be boosted by a preamplifier before anything else can be done with it. The preamplifier, usually inside the audio interface, has a knob that should be adjusted so that the amplitude is raised as much as possible without clipping, which is indicated by a red light on the interface or on the track indicator in the recording program.

Getting the right sounds in the studio gets you a long way toward a good-sounding mix. Experiment with the placement of instruments and treatment of reflecting surfaces, and the choice and placement of microphones to capture the right tone to fit the part. In Chapter 5 we will see what can be done to change tone after it has been recorded, but it is always a good idea to capture the best sounds you can from the beginning.

ACTIVITIES

Activities are suggested at three levels of difficulty to suit your system, background, and interest level. These will give you an opportunity to discover what options you have to get signals in and out of your computer, which will come in handy throughout the rest of the book.

Basic—No Equipment Required

The Basic activities can be done with either the Free or Artist version of Studio One.

Pick one or more of these activities that don't require an audio interface or microphones. The idea here is to explore options for dragging and dropping audio into Studio One without using any additional hardware.

1. See if your computer has a built-in microphone. If it does, record a track with it in Studio One of you reading something or talking about something you are interested in.

2. See if your computer has an input jack for a microphone. If it does, it may be a miniphone jack like your headphones use. If you don't have a microphone that works with it, try recording with the headphones themselves just as an

experiment. This is not what headphones are designed to do, but if yours have the right type of jack and you can plug them in, at least you'll have some way to record yourself until you can arrange for a higher-fidelity option. When you talk into the headphones, it will make the drivers vibrate, which will in turn send a voltage back down the wire.

3. Find audio files on the Internet (for example, on ccmixter.org, freesound.org, or soundclick.com), download them, and drag and drop them onto audio tracks in Studio One.

4. Figure out a workflow for recording audio on your handheld device and then transferring it to Studio One. One way to do this is to record something on your phone, upload it to SoundCloud, and then download the file on your computer and drag it into a song in Studio One. Studio One was the first DAW to offer SoundCloud integration, and PreSonus will probably continue to come up with options for integrating the network into the program. Watch this book's companion website at lovelythinking.com for updates.

5. Transfer a song from a CD onto your computer and import the audio file. You might want to get a karaoke CD if you're a singer, or a volume of Jamey Aebersold's jazz play-along recordings if you're keen on instrumental improvisation. One way to get a copy of a file off a CD is to import it into your iTunes library, which will put a copy of the song in the music folder of your computer's hard drive.

6. Search the Internet for hip-hop beats and instrumentals. Record yourself or a friend rapping over them.

7. Consider your options for getting a microphone that can plug directly into your computer instead of buying an audio interface, like a Blue Snowball USB microphone. Most of the recordings in this book were made using a PreSonus USB AudioBox or an Avid Mbox. When these audio interfaces weren't available, a portable audio/video recorder (e.g., Zoom Q2HD) was used instead.

Intermediate—Some Equipment Required

You'll need a microphone and audio interface or suitable input jack on your computer to perform the Intermediate activities.

1. Record yourself or other people using as many of the different inputs on your audio interface as you can. Try to make the recording level equally high each time. When finished, solo the tracks one at a time and compare the amplitude of the waveforms in the Arrange window with how loud they sound.

2. Do some research on different types of microphones. What brand and model do you think would be most helpful for the types of projects you are interested in? Which of the most affordable have gotten good reviews from hobbyists, industry analysts, and professional engineers? Share your sources of information with your partners.

Advanced

The Advanced activities are the most open-ended of the activities and provide jumping-off points to develop your own creative ideas.

1. Record through as many of the different inputs on your audio interface as you can. Consider creating a sense of space by placing the microphone close to (inches from) a sound source at times, and far away (several feet or more) at others. If you use original material, consider uploading to SoundCloud or another website, and posting a link to it on the discussion board area of the book's companion website, lovelythinking.com, for others to enjoy.

2. Record yourself reading a poem that has imagery that lends itself to spatial treatment.

FOR FURTHER EXPLORATION

Read:

+ Read the user's manual for your audio interface. The documentation for the AudioBox has a lot of useful information about configuring it to run with Studio One as well as a surprising amount of information on mic placement and effects.

+ *Studio One Reference Manual:* chapters on Setup and Recording. Access from within Studio One by clicking on the Help menu option at the top of the screen.

+ Bill Gibson, *Microphones & Mixers,* second edition. *Hal Leonard Recording Method,* Book 1. Montclair, NJ: Hal Leonard, 2011. Chapter 3: Mixers.

+ Bill Gibson, *Mixing & Mastering,* second edition. *Hal Leonard Recording Method,* Book 6. Montclair, NJ: Hal Leonard, 2012. See pp. 103–109 on microphone techniques.

+ Timothy Dittmar, *Audio Engineering 101: A Beginner's Guide to Music Production.* Waltham, MA: Focal Press, 2012. See pp. 47–66 on setting up microphones, and pp. 225–233 on types of cables and connectors. Review the vocabulary for this chapter with the glossary on pp. 235–237.

+ Make a bookmark in your Internet browser for Sweetwater's online glossary at www.sweetwater.com/insync/category/glossary.

Try:

+ Do some thinking about and planning for the preproduction phase of music production—the things that can be done before setting up a microphone and pressing the record button. A big part of making a good recording happens before the musicians start to play, such as having a good arrangement of a good song, good musicians who can play it well on good instruments that are in good condition, and a plan as to how the recording session will be organized.

- Make a diagram of the layout of the space you have for recording, showing the pieces of equipment you have and how they are connected to your computer. Leave enough room for performers to be comfortable and to tidy up the wiring so it's less distracting.

- Think of ways to make it easier to access your tools so that you can concentrate on making music with the time you have available.

- Have a creative spark igniter on every floor of your home, like the fire extinguishers you may have to keep the bad kind of fire from getting out of hand. Examples of these are: musical instruments, notebooks and pencils, and simple recording devices (e.g., cell phones) to capture sudden inspiration.

- Start making a list of priorities for key equipment purchases if you're interested in producing music and don't have what you need. Sales engineers at Sweetwater (sweetwater.com) are ready to match your interests and budget. Search for audio interfaces and see what the current options are.

- A sample rate of 44.1 kHz and a resolution of 16 bits are used for the projects in this book. Learn about sample rate and bit depth if you want to know how analog-to-digital conversion works and what these settings mean. We'll cover some of this in Chapter 12.

- Come up with a backup plan for your data.

QUIZ QUESTIONS

1.1: In what situations is an audio interface needed? In what situations is an audio interface not needed?

1.2: Which input on an audio interface would you plug an electric violin into? What kind of cable would you be likely to use?

1.3: Which input on an audio interface would you plug the output from a television into? What kind of cable might you use?

1.4: Looking at your audio interface while you're recording, how can you tell if you have the preamplifier level set too high?

1.5: What button do you have to press on the audio interface when using a condenser microphone? Why don't you have to press that button when using a dynamic microphone or most ribbon mics?

1.6: What is the pad switch for an audio interface? Under what circumstances would you want to use it?

1.7: Brain Buster: What can you do if the electric guitar you want to record is 20 feet from the audio interface and neither can be moved?

1.8: Imagine that you're trying to record and are not getting a signal from a condenser microphone. What is the first thing you should check, considering that you're using a condenser microphone?

1.9: If, after verifying the hardware setup in question 1.8, you're still not getting a signal, what might be wrong with the software settings?

1.10: How can you tell visually if your computer's software is receiving audio input from a microphone? What do you have to do on the computer side for this to happen?

1.11: Imagine you are trying to record someone talking with a microphone, but you aren't getting any signal at the input of your recording software. Make a list of as many things you can think of that you might check to find the cause of the problem.

1.12: How can you tell visually if you have recorded something on a track in your recording software?

1.13: Assuming you have recorded something on a track, make a list of as many things as you can think of that you might check if you don't hear anything when you try to play it back.

1.14: Brain Buster: Why might it be better to use phantom power than a battery?

1.15: Why are dynamic microphones more common onstage than condensers?

1.16: What type of microphone is a Shure SM57? What are two common uses for it in a recording studio?

1.17: What is the advantage of using condenser microphones in a studio?

1.18: What is another word for a directional pickup pattern?

1.19: Describe a situation in which an omnidirectional microphone would be better than a cardioid mic. In what situations is a cardioid mic the better choice?

1.20: What are some of the paths that indirect sound can travel before reaching your ears?

1.21: Why do room acoustics affect recordings more when microphones are set up at a greater distance from the sound source?

1.22: What is the proximity effect? What type of microphone can create it? Where does it need to be placed? What effect does it have on the sound of the recording?

1.23: Why do you need pop filters and windscreens when recording singers but not pianists?

1.24: What is the 3:1 rule?

1.25: What is phase cancellation? Why is it likely to be less noticeable if you follow the 3:1 rule?

Answers to quiz questions are in Appendix C.

STUDIO ONE SHORTCUTS

New track: T

CHAPTER 2

VOLUME

GOAL AND OBJECTIVES

After working through this chapter, you should be able to control the volume of tracks and position them in the stereo field.

- ◆ Balance the volume of multiple tracks to focus the listener's attention on the most important parts of the music.

- ◆ Use automation to change the volume of tracks over the course of a song.

- ◆ Use a compressor to automatically smooth out variations in volume and raise the overall level.

- ◆ Pan sounds between the left and right speakers.

- ◆ Explain the meaning of key vocabulary terms relating to volume.

PREREQUISITES

- ◆ Have an audio interface connected or have explored available alternatives to getting audio into your recording software (see Chapter 1).

- ◆ Understand how to record with a strong recording level (see Chapter 1).

- ◆ Have located the supplemental media (see Appendix A).

THEORY AND PRACTICE

Controlling volume is one of the most important elements in mixing. A basic introduction to acoustics is presented in this chapter to help you understand what it is and how to use software recording programs to control it effectively.

Acoustics: Amplitude and Volume

Acoustics is the study of sound and how it moves in space. Some basic information about it will help you understand the information an audio recording program displays on the screen.

Sound begins with vibrations. A vibrating body pushes and pulls on the air molecules around it, creating an alternation of pressure above and below the average pressure caused by the weight of the atmosphere above us. This alternation of higher and lower pressure creates a pressure wave that spreads out through the air. The *amplitude* is the amount of positive or negative change in air pressure measured at a point in space as the sound wave passes it. Increasing the energy of the vibrating body increases the amplitude of the pressure wave that it projects. You may be familiar with the word *amplifier*, a device that increases the amplitude of a signal to the point that it has enough energy to push and pull the cone in a loudspeaker back and forth.

When a pressure wave arrives at someone's head, it enters their ear canal and causes the eardrum at the other end to vibrate. The vibrations are then passed to the inner ear, whose hairlike cells vibrate in response and emit electrical signals that are in turn sent to the brain. The brain interprets these signals as sound. The greater the amplitude of the pressure wave, the harder the cells in the inner ear will vibrate and the louder the sound will seem to the listener.

Volume is the term musicians use to describe how loud something is. In music notation, dynamic markings are written using abbreviations for Italian words, such as *f* (for *forte*, or loud), *mf* (*mezzo forte*, or medium loud), or *pp* (*pianissimo*, or very soft). These markings are used to tell to performers how loudly they should play. This works in a group when everyone is listening to each other and adjusting their performances accordingly. When there are a lot of musicians playing together, a conductor may be needed to let them know with hand signals if they are playing too softly or loudly.

Audio engineers use a measurement system developed for electronic equipment that is more precise than the language of dynamics used by musicians. In this system, the energy of a sound is measured in decibels (dB). On one end of the decibel scale, 0 dB refers to a reference level equal to the softest sound that humans can normally hear. At the other end, 120 dB equals the "threshold of pain," an intensity level that begins to cause listeners physical pain. A volume knob on a piece of audio equipment adjusts the amplitude of the signal that comes out. Turning up the volume increases the amplitude.

Answer quiz question 2.1, found at the end of the chapter.

Microphone as Transducer

A *transducer* is a device that converts energy from one form to another. The human ear is a transducer that converts the energy in a pressure wave into an electrical signal for the brain. A loudspeaker is a transducer that converts electrical energy into magnetic energy that moves a speaker cone to drive a pressure wave into the air. A microphone is a transducer that receives a pressure wave and outputs an electrical signal whose voltage varies in a way that is analogous (similar) over time to the way the input pressure varied. That is why the signal that comes out of the microphone is called an *analog* signal.

Answer quiz question 2.2.

Waveform

The graph of changes of a microphone's output voltage over time is called a *waveform*. The horizontal axis of the graph shows the passage of time; the vertical axis indicates the amplitude. Places where the peaks are higher and the troughs are lower can be located visually. These are spots where the sound will be louder. Figure 2-1 shows a recording of two words. The word on the left was spoken at a lower volume than the word on the right, which can be heard in Audio Example 2-1.

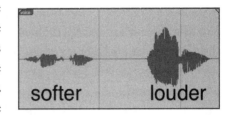

Figure 2-1. The amplitude of the word on the left has a lower amplitude.

AUDIO EXAMPLE 2-1. Playback of the soft and loud sounds.

Answer quiz question 2.3.

Normalization

There are design limits to how high the peaks can be and how low the troughs can be in a waveform passing through a piece of equipment. If the preamplifier is set too high on the audio interface while recording, the top and bottom of the waveform will be *clipped*. The flattened waveform at the points that went out of bounds is a sign of distortion.

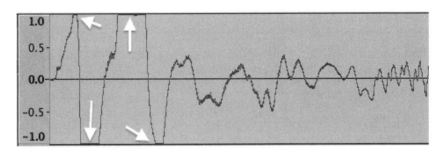

Figure 2-2. A flat waveform at the top or bottom of the range shows where the signal has been clipped. This is the beginning of the word "please" shown in Chapter 1 that was recorded without a windscreen.

The audio information in those areas that has been clipped off is lost, and the waveform cannot be fixed. Turning down the level of the clipped signal afterward makes it softer, but the flattened places in the waveform remain (Figure 2-3).

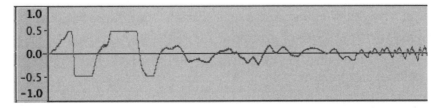

Figure 2-3. The amplitude has been reduced by decreasing the playback volume, but the distortion is still there.

Answer quiz questions 2.4 and 2.5.

It is safest to set the preamplifier level a little lower than you think necessary, in case the performer you are recording suddenly puts out more energy and surprises you with a louder-than-normal sound. If you end up with a track whose amplitude is too low and you can't rerecord it, you can boost the level afterwards. The resulting sound quality won't be quite as good as if you had recorded the track with a higher preamplifier level, but it will be better than having part of the recording clipped.

One way to boost the level of a track is a process called *normalization.* When you select a section of audio and tell the software to normalize it, the computer first reads through the audio from beginning to end to find the spot where the amplitude was the greatest, and then calculates what number that peak would have to be multiplied by to equal the maximum allowed amplitude. After this multiplying factor has been determined, the computer goes back and multiplies every point in the waveform from the beginning to the end of the section by that number. If there was any instant in the original track where the maximum volume was already reached, there won't be any change in the end, since the computer will multiply every sample by 1, which leaves all the values unchanged.

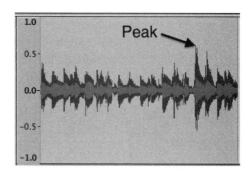

Figure 2-4. The peak value of a section of audio has been located.

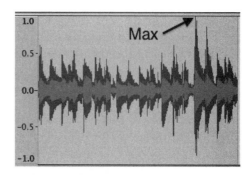

Figure 2-5. After normalizing, the previous peak amplitude has been increased to the maximum allowed.

VIDEO EXAMPLE 2-1. How to normalize a track.

EXERCISE 2-1: *Normalize the track in the too-quiet.song session file.*

Answer quiz questions 2.6 and 2.7.

Automation

In England some audio professionals have the job title of "balance engineer." In the U.S., this person is more likely to be called a recording engineer (the person who records), as opposed to a mix engineer (the person who mixes). Geoff Emerick and Norman Smith started out as balance engineers when they worked with the Beatles. The title is also very appropriate when discussing the responsibilities of a mix engineer, since balancing the volume between tracks is often more what a mix engineer is concentrating on than mixing the tracks together. In Chapter 3, your main challenge will be to balance the tracks in a song recorded in 2014 by Ken Scott, one of the other primary mix engineers who worked with the Beatles.

One advantage of the recording studio, and the reason larger facilities have multiple isolation booths, is that each instrument can be recorded on a separate track. The volume of each instrument can then be changed if necessary, independently from the rest of the group, much more easily than if all the musicians had been together in one room.

Mixing in the early days with analog tape recorders looked sometimes like a performance. Each channel on an old-school mixer has a slider called a *fader*, named for the faders on lighting boards that turn an individual light up or down on any performers in a particular area of the stage. Engineers moved the faders on the mixer up and down to control each track's volume while the song played back from the multitrack tape recorder; the stereo mix that resulted was recorded on a second tape recorder. Extra engineers were sometimes called in to lend additional pairs of hands when the mix became complicated, and the process had to be repeated as many times as necessary, or as patience and budget allowed, to make all the right moves from start to finish over the course of the song. It was hard to fix small details that were noticed during the days that followed a session, since all the controls would have to be set back up by hand to the way they had been before, and all the fader moves repeated that had been originally made correctly.

Most instruments get louder and brighter the higher they go, which is one reason songwriters usually have the melody of the chorus sung on higher notes to cut through the band and stick in the listener's memory. The opposite effect happens for low notes, which usually come out softer and duller. Listen in Audio Example 2-2 to how the vocal doesn't project as well on the low notes of the refrain ("A long way from home . . .") and gets partly covered up by the guitar, which is playing in the same register.

AUDIO EXAMPLE 2-2. The low notes of the vocal are somewhat masked by the guitar playing in the same register.

A guitarist who was listening more closely and noticed the problem could thin out the guitar part on the refrain, making it easier for the singer to be heard without pushing. This is an example of the kind of things producers and musicians work on during the preproduction phase or a recording project to simplify the mixing job and end up with a better product. Audio Example 2-3 demonstrates how much easier it is to hear the refrain when the guitarist pulls back.

AUDIO EXAMPLE 2-3. The refrain is easier to hear when the guitar thins out the guitar part.

Sometimes it is left up to engineers to fix these sorts of problems. One of the tools a computer program provides is *automation*—the storing of the operations made on the mixer's controls while listening to the song as it plays back, information that is then stored as part of the song session file. Numerous layers of automation can be recorded one by one, allowing the engineer to focus on a different aspect each time the song plays, instead of having to get everything right at once. For example, the first time through the song, the engineer could be recording changes in volume level faders on the singer's and guitarist's tracks. The next time the song is played, those fader movements will be recalled and will be automatically repeated while the volume of the drums and bass guitar can be adjusted. Automation data can be edited just like any other parameter, so you can fix one part without having to change everything else. If you decide a week later that everything is perfect except for a couple of final details, you can open up the song session file and fix just the necessary parts while leaving everything else as it sounded before.

Automation is written while playing a track back, not while it's being recorded. The track itself stays in play mode rather than record mode, so that its audio is not erased. There are five Automation Modes: off, read, touch, latch, and write.

1. **Off.** Any previously recorded automation is ignored.

2. **Read.** Plays back any previously recorded automation. It is recommended to set the Automation Mode to "off" or "read" when you don't intend to record any automation, because otherwise any adjustments you make to experiment with the settings will be recorded and subsequently repeated each time the song is played back.

3. **Touch.** Any changes you make are recorded as long as you are touching a physical control or holding down the mouse button. As soon as you let go, the setting reverts to its previously recorded position. This mode is useful if you want to make a quick adjustment, like boosting the volume of part of a solo in the middle of a section, and then let the control glide back to where it was.

4. **Latch.** Any changes are recorded until you press the stop button. You don't have to stay in contact with the controls while playback is engaged.

5. **Write.** The position of any controls writes over what was there before. This mode is often used the first time through.

Studio One stores automation data in *automation envelopes*—lines drawn between points that are created by moving the mouse. You may wish to consider adding an external hardware control surface to your setup, so that you can perform control changes using physical faders or knobs, which is more efficient and comfortable than using a mouse for everything. Automation envelopes can control any parameter you assign them to, such as volume, pan, or parameters of a virtual instrument or plug-in. They can be viewed and subsequently edited by clicking on the Show Automation icon and then choosing the parameter you wish to display. Read the *Studio One Reference Manual* section on automation envelopes for more information.

An engineer could use automation to fix the balance problem between the vocal and guitar heard in Audio Example 2-2 in order to improve the balance between the competing vocal and guitar tracks. The process of recording automation is demonstrated in Video Example 2-2. The improved balance that results can be heard in Audio Example 2-4.

VIDEO EXAMPLE 2-2. How to record and edit automation.

AUDIO EXAMPLE 2-4. The vocal can be heard better after automating the volume levels.

EXERCISE 2-2: *Record automation for the vocal and guitar tracks in the automate.song session file.*

Answer quiz questions 2.8 and 2.9.

Fade-Ins and Fade-Outs

Gradually turning up the volume of a track is called *fading in*. *Fading out* is the opposite process: gradually reducing the amplitude of a signal. Both terms are inherited from the film industry. In the early days, filmmakers were afraid to cut from one scene directly to another because they thought it might confuse the audience, so they would fade to black before switching scenes. Fade-outs are sometimes used in songs to give the impression that the musicians are continuing to play off into the distance even after the song ends. The last line of the final chorus in Adam Ezra's "Sacred Ground" is repeated and gradually faded out. Figure 2-6 shows how such a fade-out gradually decreases the amplitude of the waveform of the resulting mix (Audio Example 2-5). The process is demonstrated in Video Example 2-3.

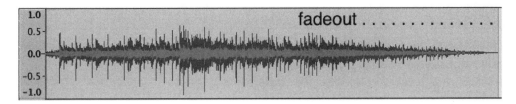

Figure 2-6. The waveform of the fade-out gradually goes down to 0.

AUDIO EXAMPLE 2-5. The ending vamp is faded out.

VIDEO EXAMPLE 2-3. How to create a fade-out by automating the master fader.

EXERCISE 2-3: *Automate a fade-out at the end of the song in session fadeout.song.*

Answer quiz question 2.10.

Compression

The word *compression* has a number of meanings in music production. The first relates to acoustics (see Chapter 1) and describes an increase in pressure that air molecules can undergo. The times when air pressure is high are represented by peaks or high points in the graph of a waveform. The opposite of this type of compression is *rarefaction*—when air molecules are pulled apart and air pressure drops below normal. These times are indicated in the graph of waveform as dips or *troughs*.

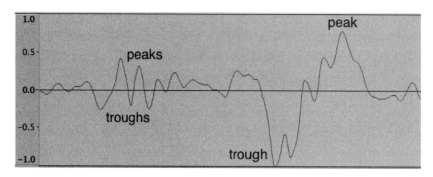

Figure 2-7. Peaks and troughs in a waveform caused by compression and rarefaction.

A second meaning of the word compression is in regard to *data compression*. This comes into play when converting full-fidelity WAV or AIFF audio file to a smaller file in MP3 format. This type of compression will be covered in Chapter 12.

The type of compression that interests us in this chapter is *audio compression*, a process that automatically controls volume. Audio compression turns down the loudest parts of a track and saves the engineer from having to automate volume control by hand.

Let's create an imaginary human drama to help us understand what the four controls of a compressor do. Imagine a grandmother or another trusted family member who has assumed responsibility for regulating the volume of the audio system in the living room, where she sits with her hand on the volume knob with her mind set on what the maximum volume level of the music should be. That volume level is called the *threshold level*. Once the amplitude of the signal coming into the amplifier gets louder than the level she has set for the threshold, she automatically turns the volume knob down, reducing the level of what goes out the loudspeakers.

Let's imagine Grandmother is feeling fine today, and we're playing a song that she likes. In this case, she sets the threshold fairly high (Figure 2-8), indicating that she will react to turn down only the very loudest parts of the song. Notice that only the peak amplitudes of the waveform go beyond the threshold volume level she has settled on (Figure 2-9). These are the parts that will be turned down. Adjusting the threshold to suit the volume levels of the input is demonstrated in Video Example 2-4.

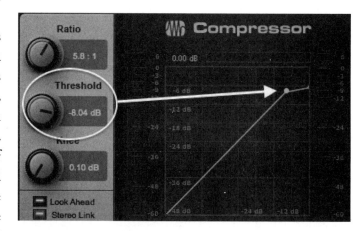

Figure 2-8. Settings for a compressor set with a high threshold. Notice the position of the threshold control and its effect on the breakpoint in the graph.

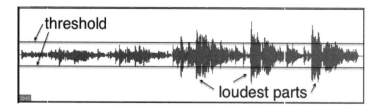

Figure 2-9. Only the loudest parts of the input waveform exceed the threshold set for the compressor.

VIDEO EXAMPLE 2-4. Setting the threshold of the compressor so that it is activated only for the peaks of the signal.

EXERCISE 2-4: *Set a level for the threshold in the compressor.song session so that the compressor is activated only for the peak amplitudes.*

Later in the day, Grandmother becomes annoyed with us, partly because we keep playing the same song over and over again. As a result, she now has a lower threshold of tolerance (Figure 2-10), and will turn the music down anytime it gets above medium loud (Figure 2-11). Since the input from the whole song is mostly medium loud or louder, she will be turning it down most of the time. Video Example 2-5 shows how this situation would be set up with a compressor and the resulting sound.

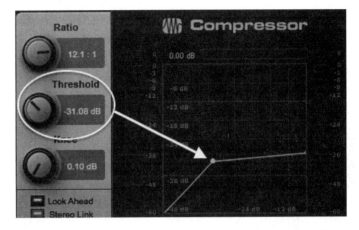

Figure 2-10. Settings for a compressor set with a lower threshold. Notice the new position of the threshold control.

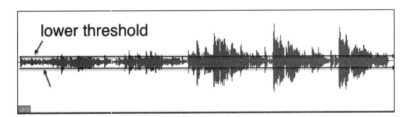

Figure 2-11. The original input waveform with the new lower threshold level superimposed. Notice that the amplitude of most of the song is now above the threshold.

What the compressor does is reduce the volume of just the parts that exceed the threshold. Notice in Figure 2-12 that the soft parts—those below the threshold—have been left alone, and only the loud parts have been turned down.

Figure 2-12. Everything above the threshold level has been reduced.

VIDEO EXAMPLE 2-5. Raising a compressor's output gain.

EXERCISE 2-5: *Raise the output level in the compressor.song session.*

Two other main parameters affect the compressor. While Grandmother's wisdom has grown over time, her response time has become somewhat impaired. There is a period of time between when she notices that the input level has exceeded the threshold and when she reacts and turns the volume down. We call this the *attack time*. The amount of time it takes for her to notice that the music input level has dropped back down below the threshold and turn the volume back up is called the *release time*.

Hopefully, thinking about a real-world analogy helped you visualize how compression works. Let's send Grandmother off to find something more enjoyable to do, while we review how a compressor works by seeing how it could take over her job. A compressor is a device used for automatic volume control, saving the engineer from having to automate changes in volume over the course of an entire song. It turns down the loudest parts, leaving the softest parts alone. This reduces the *dynamic range*, since there is less difference in amplitude between the softest and loudest parts of a track.

One application of a compressor is to raise the volume of quiet passages in music, to make it possible to hear them in noisy environments like cars. If the engineer simply raises the volume of the input to make the very soft parts louder, then the parts that were already very loud will get louder as well, and cause distortion since the speakers cannot handle them, as shown in Figure 2-13.

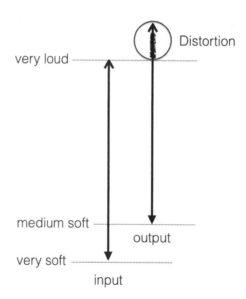

Figure 2-13. Turning up everything to make the very softest parts audible will cause the very loudest parts to distort.

The compressor can help avoid this by first turning down the very loudest parts of the input, so that they are only medium loud. The whole compressed signal can then be boosted—the very softest parts will become medium loud, and the very loudest parts will go back to where they originally were. This process is shown in Figure 2-14.

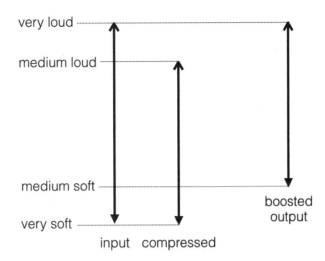

Figure 2-14. Boosting the compressed signal raises the very softest sounds without distorting the very loudest parts.

The first thing to adjust when using a compressor is the threshold level. This can be done by locating the loudest parts in a track and then setting the threshold level so that it is below the level of the peaks. Anytime the input level to the compressor goes above the threshold, the compressor will be activated. Setting the threshold level too low will activate the compressor too often.

The attack time control in the compressor sets the amount of time it takes for the compressor to actually start turning the level down once the input level has exceeded the threshold. If the attack time is very short, the short transient sounds that help the listener identify which instrument is playing will be turned down. Cutting off the initial attack of a sound doesn't help reduce the overall gain much. What is more helpful is to reduce the level of the steady sustained section, if there is one.

The compression ratio is expressed as a ratio—two numbers separated by a colon. The number on the left side indicates how many dB the input has to increase to cause a 1 dB increase in the output—3 to 1 is fairly mild, whereas 12 to 1 is severe. A compressor with a ratio of infinity to 1 is called a *limiter*, since it sets a hard level above which the output will never go.

The release time of a compressor refers to how long it takes for the compressor to stop turning down the sound after the input signal level drops back below the threshold level. As with the attack time, sudden changes of dynamics may not be desirable, so you may not want to set the release time too low.

Answer quiz questions 2.11–2.14.

Tremolo is another effect that can be used to automatically control volume. Whereas *vibrato* creates a repeated pattern of increase and decrease of pitch/frequency (Audio Example 2-6), tremolo causes a series of high and low amplitudes (Figure 2-15, Audio Example 2-7).

AUDIO EXAMPLE 2-6. Vibrato repeatedly changes pitch.

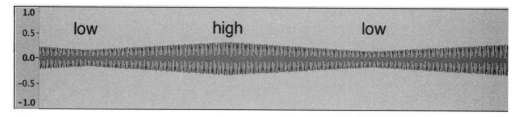

Figure 2-15. A recording of a guitar with a tremolo effect.

AUDIO EXAMPLE 2-7. Tremolo repeatedly changes volume.

In Studio One, tremolo is done with the X-Trem plug-in. Figure 2-16 shows its controls for depth (intensity of volume change), speed (how rapidly the volume is changed), pan (on stereo tracks), and LFO mode (shape of modulating wave), allowing for syncing with the tempo of the music. Video Example 2-6 shows the process of adding tremolo to the recording of an electric guitar.

Figure 2-16. The X-Trem plug-in.

VIDEO EXAMPLE 2-6. Adjusting the parameters of the X-Trem plug-in.

EXERCISE 2-6: *Experiment with the tremolo settings in the tremolo.song session file.*

You will need to save your mix to a file anytime you want to hear your work outside of Studio One. This process is called exporting and is demonstrated in Video Example 2-7.

VIDEO EXAMPLE 2-7. Export your mix so you can play it outside of Studio One.

EXERCISE 2-7: *Export your work with the tremolo.song.*

Answer quiz question 2.15.

Panning

The last topic in this chapter on controlling volume is *panning*. Like fading in and out, panning is a term that comes from the film industry, short for "panoramic"—an effect where the camera sweeps from one side of a scene to another. Since the inception of stereo audio reproduction, it has been possible to simulate the position of a sound by sending the track to both output channels with different volume levels. If you want the sound to appear to come out of the left speaker, then you send the full volume of the track to the left side and none to the right. If you want it to seem to come from the center, you send it at equal volume to both speakers. If you want it somewhat right of center, then you send it at a medium-loud level through the right speaker and a medium-soft level through the left.

Monophonic (or *mono*) means the same sound comes out of both speakers or out of the one speaker found on some televisions and radios. Stereophonic (or *stereo*) sound provides the option of using pan controls to separate tracks in the stereo field, thereby opening up space for each instrument to be heard.

The bass frequencies in low-pitched sounds spread out from the loudspeakers and fill the room, making it hard to know which speaker they are coming from, so there is not much point to panning them to one side or the other. For this reason, the bass guitar and kick drum are usually panned to the center position, along with other tracks like lead vocals that are meant to be the focus of the listener's attention. Compare the difference in panning effects depending on frequency in Audio Example 2-8, in which a low-pitched sound is first sent out only through the left channel, and then equally from both channels, and then from the right channel only. Next, a high-pitched sound follows the same left-center-right path. The choice of whether to listen on headphones or over loudspeakers will also affect the experience.

AUDIO EXAMPLE 2-8. A test of panning.

Start paying attention to the difference in panning effects created by loudspeakers compared with headphones. Spatial effects are easier to control for a listener wearing headphones, because the left ear hears only the left channel, while the right hears only the right channel. An engineer has less control over the how the listener experiences panning effects when the music is being played through loudspeakers, since the signal level that each of the ears receives from each speaker depends on the listener's position in the room relative to the location of the loudspeakers.

Video Example 2-8 shows how tracks are assigned to the left, center, and right positions. Notice how the relative amplitudes of the left and right channels change on the meters of the main stereo output when the pan slider is adjusted, and how locations of low-pitched sounds are not as clear as the high-pitched ones when played through loudspeakers.

VIDEO EXAMPLE 2-8. Pan sliders control the locations of low- and high-pitched sounds in the stereo field.

EXERCISE 2-8: *Change the panning in the pan-experiment.song session file. Compare the effects when wearing earphones with listening through loudspeakers.*

Answer quiz questions 2.16–2.21.

REVIEW

The study of acoustics helps us understand how sound waves behave. Vibrating objects cause pressure waves to spread out into a space, and microphones convert changes in air pressure as they pass to changes in voltage. A waveform is a graph of the changes in voltage over time, and the height above and below the centerline of the waveform graph represents the wave's amplitude. The louder the sound in the air, the bigger its amplitude when graphed as a waveform. The intensity of sounds is measured in decibels (dB).

Recording software offers the user a number of options for controlling the amplitude of an audio signal. The position of the fader for a track can be automated to turn the tracks' volume up and down automatically each time the song is played back.

Another way to control the amplitude of a signal is by running it through a compressor, which turns down the volume each time the signal gets louder than a preset threshold. The signal ends up with a more consistent volume as a result of reducing the dynamic range, keeping the loudest notes from sticking out.

Panning can be used to spread out instruments in the stereo field and make the individual parts more noticeable.

The techniques for volume control explored in this chapter will be applied in the next chapter, in which you will mix a larger group of instruments playing a whole song.

ACTIVITIES

Activities are suggested at three different levels, making it easier for you to find a way to practice the techniques presented in the "Theory and Practice" section that is appropriate to your background and interest level, and the equipment you have at your disposal. The Basic activities depend only on having a computer with a version of Studio One Free or Artist installed on it. No microphone or audio interface is necessary, and the steps required to perform them are relatively simple. The Intermediate activities are a bit more challenging and in many cases depend on having an audio interface and microphone. The Advanced activities are the most open-ended and invite you to exercise your imagination and creativity. Post links to your responses to these on the discussion board on the book's companion website at lovelythinking.com.

Basic

1. Set the level for the each of the faders on the motherless-child.song session to achieve a balanced sound. Check the levels of the master fader while you are playing the song to see that the combination of the sound from each of the tracks adds up consistently around the −3 dB to −6 dB lines. Leave the pan sliders in the center position and export the mix in mono, using the name motherless-child-mono. Try panning one guitar mostly to the left (around L54) and the other guitar mostly to the right (around R54) and listen to the effect. Try other positions and see which you like better. Now pan one *hard left*, or all the way to the left (L), and the other *hard right*, or all the way to the right (R). Export the mix with the name motherless-child-stereo. Play both mixes back with your computer's music player (Windows Media Player on a PC, or iTunes or QuickTime Player on a Mac). Which mix do you prefer? Why?

Intermediate

1. Record three tracks. Compare the effect of panning each track to one of three positions—hard left (L), center (0), and hard right (R)—with moving them closer to the center, by panning the tracks partway to the left (L54), center (0), and partway to the right (R54).

2. Record yourself or someone else talking, singing, or playing one or more instruments on three tracks. Listen to headphones while recording the second and third tracks, so that they combine well with what has been previously recorded. Adjust the faders so that all three tracks start out about equally loud, and then automate the volume level of any track that varies significantly. Consider automating the level of one or more of the faders for dramatic effect.

   After you have the volumes set the way you want, pan the tracks apart—one track hard left, one in the center, and one hard right. Notice whether working with a reduced number of options stimulates your creativity. Export the recording using the name L-C-R.wav. After listening to this effect, try panning the three tracks to different locations and decide which arrangement you like the best. Export the new recording with the name my-panning.wav.

   Automate the Main fader to fade in at the beginning of your recording and fade out at the end. Export the mix with the name with-fades.wav.

   Listen to your three versions. Take notes on the effects you used and which you liked best.

Advanced

1. Record several tracks of yourself or other people. Encourage the performers to create sounds at a wide range of dynamic levels. Set a starting amplitude using the fader for each track and then automate changes in the fader over time while you react to the changes in amplitude of the performances. Automate the panning of one or more tracks. Export the stereo mix with the name automate-volume-and-panning.wav.

2. Experiment with inserting a compressor plug-in on a track that has a wide dynamic range to reduce the amplitude of the peaks automatically, rather than automating the volume fader. Make up for the drop in volume by turning up the plug-in's output gain. Keep the result below 0 dB on the Main Out fader.

3. Experiment with PreSonus's X-Trem tremolo/autopanner plug-in with tempo sync and step-sequence modulation.

FOR FURTHER EXPLORATION

Read:

- *Studio One Reference Manual* on Automation/Track Automation.
- Bill Gibson, *Microphones & Mixers*, second edition. *Hal Leonard Recording Method*, Book 1. Montclair, NJ: Hal Leonard, 2011. Chapter 1: Sound Theory.
- Bill Gibson, *Mixing & Mastering*, second edition. *Hal Leonard Recording Method*, Book 6. Montclair, NJ: Hal Leonard, 2012. See pp. 99–103 and 110–114 on panning. Chapter 7 (pp. 163–192) covers automation in more detail.
- Roey Izhaki, *Mixing Audio: Concepts, Practices and Tools*. Waltham, MA: Focal Press, 2012. Chapters 15 and 16 on compression.

Investigate:

- Putting musicians in separate booths and playing with headphones isolates them from each other, making it harder to naturally balance their volumes. Try putting people in the same room without headphones. Look for people to record who listen well to each other and leave space for parts to come through, so that you don't have to do so much automation afterward.
- There's only so much that engineer can do with a volume slider on the mixer. The next time you have a recording session, see if the performers are thinning out what they are playing, and/or changing registers at certain places in the song, and/or adjusting their volume levels to let all the parts be heard. How does it affect the mix if this is or isn't happening?
- Find out how you can conserve your hearing. Most regulatory agencies like OSHA recommend that workers not be subjected to an average of more than 85 dB during an eight-hour workday, to avoid long-term damage to hearing from noise exposure. For every 3 dB increase in sound level above 85 dB, the recommended listening time goes down by half. Loud sporting events (105 dB) are safe for less than 23 minutes per week. Learn about where the sounds you are surrounded by fall on the dB scale. The range covers sounds from a pin dropping (approximately 10 dB) to a toilet flushing (75 dB), a motorcycle (100 dB), a rock band (110 dB), an emergency vehicle siren (115 dB), a balloon popping (125 dB), a shotgun (160 dB) and a rocket launch (180 dB). At 194 dB, sound waves turn into shock waves. Consider getting a device (or an app for your phone) to measure sound pressure levels in order to become able to identify levels that are dangerously high, and to protect yourself with hearing protection devices when necessary.

QUIZ QUESTIONS

2.1: What are the units of measurement that engineers use to describe the volume of a sound?

2.2: What does a transducer do?

2.3: What does the graph of a waveform show you?

2.4: What causes clipping? What can be done to avoid it?

2.5: Describe the waveform shown in Figure 2-17. Which of the words labeled A, B, or C looks the best of the three for a recording? Why?

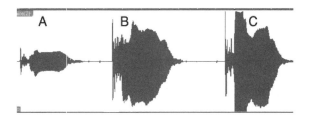

Figure 2-17.

2.6: What does normalizing do to a track?

2.7: Brain Buster: Imagine you've recorded a track and part of it has clipped, which you can observe by looking at the waveform and noticing that at some points, the tops and bottoms are flat where the original signal exceeded the maximum amplitude level. How will the waveform be changed, if at all, if you normalize it? Why?

2.8: What purpose does automation serve?

2.9: What are automation envelopes? Where can you find them on the screen in Studio One?

2.10: How do you make a track fade out?

2.11: Explain what threshold, attack time, release time, and ratio controls do in a compressor.

2.12: How do compressors reduce the dynamic range of a track?

2.13: Brain Buster: Which type of music is most likely to benefit from compression: heavy metal or classical orchestra music? Why?

2.14: Brain Buster: Why is turning up a track after it's been compressed less likely to distort it than turning up the same track without having compressed it?

2.15: What's the difference between tremolo and vibrato?

2.16: What is *acoustics* the study of?

2.17: Explain the sequence of events starting with the energy in the vibrations of a string and ending with the sound resolving in a listener's brain.

2.18: What does the *amplitude* of a waveform refer to? What effect does increasing the amplitude have on the sound? What knob on a stereo system or TV controls the amplitude of the audio?

2.19: What is a *transducer*? In what way does a flashlight act as a transducer? How about the pickups on an electric guitar? An internal combustion engine? The human eye?

2.20: What is the unit of measure for the amplitude or volume of a sound?

2.21: Brain Buster: Panning is usually done on a single audio track by adjusting its pan pot (knob or slider) on the mixing board. To make the sound come out of the left speaker, you turn the pan pot all the way to the left. Now imagine that you have same sound playing through two tracks on the mixer instead of one—with one track assigned to the left output channel and the other track assigned to the right output channel—and these two tracks have faders but no pan pots. How would you set the faders for the two tracks to make the sound come out of only the left side? How would adjust them, then, if you wanted the sound to seem to come out of the middle?

Answers to quiz questions are in Appendix C.

CHAPTER 3

MIXING WITH VOLUME

GOAL AND OBJECTIVES

After working through this chapter, you should be able to use volume controls to effectively balance tracks.

+ Control the relative volume of tracks in a medium-size session.

+ Change volume over the duration of the song.

+ Use panning and doubling to affect sense of space.

+ Organize tracks to make layout easier to understand.

+ Apply plug-ins to the main mix.

PREREQUISITES

+ Review concepts introduced in Chapter 2, such as how to automate volume changes, apply compression, and pan tracks in the stereo field.

THEORY AND PRACTICE

In Chapter 2, we developed some techniques to control the volume of tracks, beginning with recording a strong signal from a microphone. We also saw how to control the playback level of those tracks—either by hand, by automating their fader levels; or by using a compression plug-in to reduce the dynamic range. Panning a track to one side of the stereo field was shown to be a special type of volume control, achieved by turning it up louder in one speaker than another.

In this chapter, we will apply those techniques, starting with setting a basic balance between tracks. We will then look at how mixing can modify the texture of a recording and temporarily shift the listener's focus over the course of a song. Learning how to organize track layout and create submixes to make it easier to focus on specific tasks will make mixing larger sessions more understandable and efficient. At the end of the chapter, you'll have the opportunity to mix "Easy Street," a song recorded by Ken Scott, one of the principal engineers to work with the Beatles, and to see how he doubled vocal and guitar parts.

Basic Balance

One of the first things to do when recording and mixing a song is to form an idea of the functions of the various parts. How important is each element? If you think of the song as a story, what role does each instrument play? Which instruments are leading actors, and which are the supporting cast? You may wish to place microphones closer to the instruments that are meant to be in front, in order to get the clearest sound, and then turn them up a bit in the mix. Becoming familiar with the lyrics and their meaning can help guide you in deciding how understandable the words should be, and the prominence the vocal deserves in the mix.

The drum set itself is made up of a number of instruments—kick and snare drums, one or more tom-toms, and the hi-hat, crash, and ride cymbals. Normally, more than one microphone is used for the drum set: one for the kick, one on the snare, one on the hi-hat, and a raised *stereo pair* to pick up the other cymbals and the rest of the kit. Sometimes additional microphones are set up for the tom-toms. Since the drums setup is often the most complicated, one of the first orders of business is to find a good balance for its various tracks.

There are a variety of balancing strategies that can be used to find basic volume settings for a mix. They fall into two basic categories: additive and subtractive. The additive approach is to start with all the faders turned down, and then to turn them up one by one. One way to do this with the drum set would be to start with the kick drum and snare drums, and then turn up any additional drum or hi-hat mics, and then add the overhead mics to get the raised cymbals (Video Example 3-1).

VIDEO EXAMPLE 3-1. An additive approach to mixing the drums starting with the kick and snare.

EXERCISE 3-1: *Mix the drum set in the drum-balance.song session file, starting with the kick and snare.*

An additive mix could also begin in the opposite order, starting with the overheads, which pick up sound from the whole kit, and then adding the individual mics as needed to increase power and definition (Video Example 3-2). Since the overhead drum mics are usually recorded with a stereo pair, you may wish to start with panning them apart, keeping the kick drum in the center, and then panning the snare and tom mics to match where they sit in the stereo field created by the overhead mics (Figure 3-1).

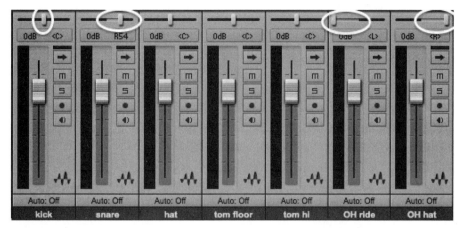

Figure 3-1. The overhead mics are panned all the way to left and right. The kick is placed in the center and the snare to the right, as it usually is if we are facing the drum set.

VIDEO EXAMPLE 3-2. An additive approach to mixing the drums starting with the overheads.

EXERCISE 3-2: *Mix the drum set in the drum-balance.song session file, starting with the overheads.*

Panning the overheads as wide as possible (i.e., *hard left* and *hard right*) may not sound natural, since the audience is usually not sitting close enough to the drums to hear so much separation.

VIDEO EXAMPLE 3-3. Panning the drum mics closer to the center, and then all the way to the center so that they become mono.

EXERCISE 3-3: *Reduce the degree of panning of the drum set mics in the drum-balance.song session file.*

Compare the three different versions:

AUDIO EXAMPLE 3-1. Wide stereo.

AUDIO EXAMPLE 3-2. Narrow stereo.

AUDIO EXAMPLE 3.3. Mono mix.

The drum set we've been working with was recorded with seven microphones. The signal path diagrammed in Figure 3-2 shows that the output of the individual drum tracks are routed to the Console's main outputs.

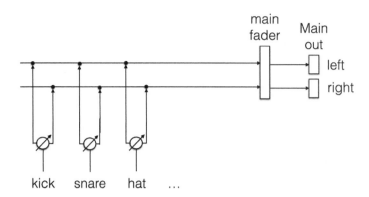

Figure 3-2. The output of each drum track is connected to the main outputs.

At some point as the number of tracks grows in a session, there will be more tracks than can be viewed in one window, and the engineer will have to scroll right and left to see everything. One way to reduce the amount of information on the screen is to take advantage of Studio One's folder feature, which helps group related tracks. Video Example 3-4 shows how individual tracks can be dragged into a folder track in the Arrangement window (Figure 3-3).

Once the folder is closed, the individual drum tracks are hidden (Figure 3-4).

Submix

The power of folder tracks can be extended by creating a *submix* for the individual drum tracks. A submix is used to mix two or more tracks into one signal, which is routed through a *bus* channel—a virtual wire that runs through the mixer. The bus shows up on the mixer in a single channel whose amplitude can be controlled with one fader. After the submix has been created, the original tracks going into the Console can be hidden from view, reducing the amount of information the engineer has to deal with and making it possible to see everything necessary in a single window. This does more than just reduce the clutter on

Figure 3-3. A folder track holding seven drum tracks.

Figure 3-4. The closed drums folder track.

the screen. Once a balance of volumes of the individual drum mics has been set, the entire kit can be turned up and down with a single fader, while keeping the relative balance between them.

Creating the submix is easy once you have a folder track created with the individual audio tracks in it. Look under the name of the folder and click on the word None, and then choose the Add Bus Channel option (Figure 3-5). Each bus channel appears in the Console window as a single fader.

Figure 3-5. Creating a bus channel.

Figure 3-6 shows the new signal flow for the drum tracks whose outputs are now being combined in a bus channel. The bus channel is then fed into the main mix bus. Notice that the labeling of the outputs has changed in the Console view (Figure 3-7).

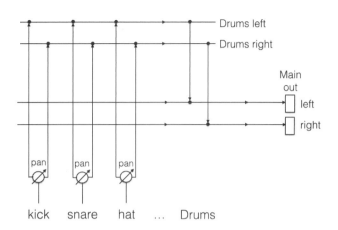

Figure 3-6. A diagram of the signal flow showing how the outputs of the drum tracks are connected to the Drums submix.

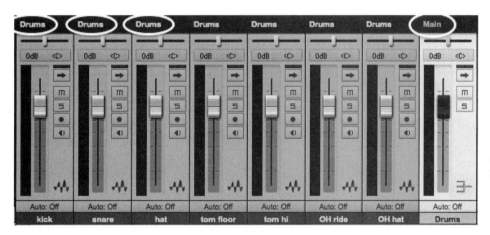

Figure 3-7. The Drum submix is connected to the main outs.

Clicking on the Banks button to the left of the Console window opens a list of the tracks that appear in the Console view. Clicking on the name of each individual drum track grays it out and removes it from the Console (Figure 3-8). Video Example 3-4 shows this process.

VIDEO EXAMPLE 3-4. How to create a new folder and bus channel to make a submix.

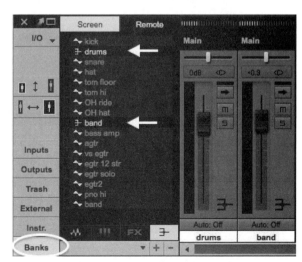

Figure 3-8. The tracks of individual drums with grayed-out names are hidden in the Console view.

EXERCISE 3-4: *Create a new folder and bus channel for the drums in the drum-balance.song session file.*

The additive and subtractive approaches used in creating a drum submix can be applied to the whole mix. In the additive approach, faders are turned up one by one as much as necessary to make each track loud enough in the mix. A balance engineer's artistry begins with knowing just what that means for each track, and depends to a great degree on how important the part is to the song and where it sits in the frequency range, as will be discussed in Chapter 5. Some engineers prefer to start with the rhythm section and then gradually bring up the rest of the group. Let's try this approach to find a balance between some of the individual instruments in the band and our drum submix, as demonstrated in Video Example 3-5.

VIDEO EXAMPLE 3-5. Start with the rhythm section to set the groove.

EXERCISE 3-5: *Start with the rhythm section in the adam-ezra.song session file.*

Another additive approach is to begin with the lead vocal and then add the support.

VIDEO EXAMPLE 3-6. Start with the lead vocal.

EXERCISE 3-6: *Start the mix with the lead vocal.*

The subtractive method takes the opposite approach: You start with all the faders turned up, and then turn down the less important parts until a proper balance is achieved. This is like what a sculptor does, starting with a block of rock and then chipping away the pieces that don't belong.

VIDEO EXAMPLE 3-7. Mixing the same tracks using the subtractive approach.

EXERCISE 3-7: *Gradually turn down the instruments enough to be able to hear the vocal clearly.*

Answer quiz question 3.1, found at the end of the chapter.

Texture

The *texture* of a piece of music refers to its overall quality, generated from a combination of melody, rhythm, and harmony. The process of mixing can affect the texture of a song, as the thickness and prominence of the various tracks are adjusted. The most common texture in popular music today is a lead vocal with background accompaniment. Listen to Audio Example 3-4 and take notes on which parts are the most noticeable because of their variety or volume, and which parts are more in the background. Pay special attention to how much the lead vocal stands out.

AUDIO EXAMPLE 3-4. Stereo mix of "Easy Street."

Answer quiz questions 3.2–3.4.

Mixing engineers usually make adjustments to the volume of the tracks over the course of the song, rather than setting a basic balance and leaving it for an entire song. Listen to the ending of Adam Ezra's "Sacred Ground" (Audio Example 3-5). Note how after ten seconds the lyrics run out and the vocal gets softer, making the slide guitar stand out. More reverb is added to move the music back, after which it fades out. Changes like these help maintain the listener's attention and interest.

AUDIO EXAMPLE 3-5. The lead vocal and slide guitar exchange positions at the end.

Answer quiz question 3.5.

Doubling

Doubling is the process of combining two versions of a signal to create a richer sound. One way to get the two signals from a single instrument is with a direct injection (DI) box, as explained in Chapter 1. These devices allow the signal coming from a guitar or bass to be divided into two. One of the outputs is plugged into an instrument amplifier and can be recorded with a microphone. The second output can be connected to a microphone input on the audio interface, using a microphone cable, and is usually the brighter of the two. Compare the sound of the two bass tracks recorded for "Easy Street," the first (Audio Example 3-6) recorded with a microphone on the bass amp and the second (Audio Example 3-7) recorded simultaneously with a DI box. The process of mixing the two together is demonstrated in Video Example 3-8.

AUDIO EXAMPLE 3-6. Bass amp recorded with microphone.

AUDIO EXAMPLE 3-7. Bass through a DI box.

VIDEO EXAMPLE 3-8. Mixing microphone and DI bass tracks.

EXERCISE 3-8: *Experiment with blending the mic and DI tracks in the basses.song session file.*

One way to double percussion sounds is with drum replacement. This allows you to replace the drum sounds you have recorded with others made by professional engineers using a variety of microphones, rooms, and models of instruments. For "Easy Street," the engineers decided to augment the kick and snare tracks with sampled instruments. Audio Example 3-8 is of the drummer's kick drum, Audio Example 3-9 is of the recorded kick drum sample, and Audio Example 3-10 shows what the two sound like at equal volumes. As with the layering of the bass amp and DI tracks, combining recorded and sampled sounds—or replacing the recorded sounds completely—opens up new tonal possibilities. Video Example 3-9 shows how this is done.

AUDIO EXAMPLE 3-8. The natural kick drum sound.

AUDIO EXAMPLE 3-9. The same track triggering a kick drum sample.

AUDIO EXAMPLE 3-10. The natural and sampled sounds layered together.

VIDEO EXAMPLE 3-9. How to blend natural and sampled sounds.

EXERCISE 3-9: *Balance the kick and snare tracks with their related samples in the samples. song file.*

The most popular way since the 1960s to make a vocal or instrumental hook stand out is to double it, overdubbing the same part on a new track to thicken the texture. Many of the parts in "Easy Street" have been doubled.

VIDEO EXAMPLE 3-10. Working with the doubled tracks in "Easy Street."

EXERCISE 3-10: *Balance the doubled guitars in the doubles.song session.*

Answer quiz questions 3.6–3.8.

Panning

Panning doubled parts to opposite sides of the stereo field widens the image (Audio Examples 3-11 and 3-12).

AUDIO EXAMPLE 3-11. Two guitar tracks in mono.

AUDIO EXAMPLE 3-12. A wider image is achieved by panning them apart.

Most of the tracks in the studio mix of "Easy Street" were panned to the center. The doubled electric guitar part (vs egtr and vs egtr db) that begins in the second verse and the electric guitar solo (egtr solo and egtr solo dbl) that comes in after the bridge were panned apart, as shown in Video Example 3-10.

Fills

Another element in a song's texture are the *fills* that may be played in gaps in the vocal lines. Listen in Audio Example 3-13 to how pianist Alfredo Cardim demonstrates this technique when his left hand plays most of his chords and counterlines in between the melody and solo his right hand is playing. Musicians who do this reduce the amount of automation that will have to be done during the mixing phase, leaving the engineer free to concentrate on other issues, such as how loud the acoustic guitarist's track should be to maintain the groove and support the harmony.

AUDIO EXAMPLE 3-13. A quartet playing Alfredo Cardim's "Evening in Copacabana."

Describe the balance between the instruments. What is the function of the acoustic guitar? Can you hear the brushes on the hi-hat cymbals playing the steady sixteenth notes? What do you think about the volume of the syncopated snare-drum rim shots? Being familiar with the style, in this case bossa nova, helps in making this sort of decision. When in doubt, compare your mixes to reference recordings—classics in the style of music you're working on. The song should be counted with two beats per bar. Can you hear the bass player's half notes clearly enough? It establishes the basic pulse around which everything else revolves. You'll have a chance to mix this song in Chapter 9.

In pop song recordings, specific tracks are often assigned to record fills and other supporting parts to make the texture more interesting, something the producer may become involved with to pump up a track. Sometimes these take the form of an instrumental hook, such as what's heard between verses in "Easy Street" (Audio Example 3-14). The engineer needs to decide how loud to make these parts (Video Example 3-11).

AUDIO EXAMPLE 3-14. Overemphasized instrumental hook in "Easy Street."

VIDEO EXAMPLE 3-11. Finding the right balance for a guitar fill.

EXERCISE 3-11: *Experiment with the level of the guitar fill in guitar-fill.song.*

The same type of fills can be heard in Sam Broussard's "Times Like These" (Audio Example 3-15), which you'll have a chance to mix in Chapter 7. Notice the acoustic guitar instrumental hook and the fretless bass fill during the verse, and how the instruments leave space for his voice to come through.

AUDIO EXAMPLE 3-15. "Times Like These."

Organizing for Understanding and Efficiency

The session files you've worked with so far in the book have had only a few tracks. This chapter gives you the opportunity to concentrate on controlling the balance in a larger session. The more tracks you have in a session, the more confusing and unwieldy mixing can become. Fortunately, there are a number of things that can be done to simplify how things are laid out on the screen, making it easier to see what is going on and to get to the controls you need to use quickly, which will help you concentrate on finding a good balance for the tracks. We have already seen how folders can hold a group of tracks and that submixes occupy only one fader in the Console mixer view. There are other tools to maximize the use of screen space, and using a consistent layout, adding visual cues, and documenting what's there can help increase efficiency.

The best way to increase the capacity of the Console mix view is to pop it out of the window it usually shares at the bottom of the Arrange window (Video Example 3-12). This is especially powerful if you have two monitors, since the Arrange window can be put in one and the Console in the other. Giving tracks short, informative names makes it easier to find the one you need while you're mixing. Switching in the Console from wide to narrow video increases the number of tracks you can see in one window, but the trade-off is that it reduces the length of the names that can be shown.

VIDEO EXAMPLE 3-12. Clicking on the pop-out icon opens up the Console in a separate window.

EXERCISE 3-12: *Pop the Console window out and rename the tracks in the pop-out-console.song session file.*

The "Easy Street" session files in this chapter use colors to make the grouping of related tracks easier to perceive. The drums are dark blue; the bass tracks are brown; the acoustic guitars are green; the electric guitars, 12-string guitar, and mandolin are blue; the background vocals are light green; and the lead vocals are orange. You may want to develop your own system of colors and intensities that makes sense to you. Some people use red and yellow for hot tracks, blue or green for cooler sounds, brown for rugged foundations, and black for those that should be muted when mixing. Video Example 3-13 shows how to pick colors for tracks.

VIDEO EXAMPLE 3-13. Assigning colors to tracks.

EXERCISE 3-13: *Assign colors to the tracks in the pop-out-console.song session.*

Another way to make it easier to deal with a larger number of tracks is by having a consistent left-to-right order in the Console view. One standard layout starts with the kick and snare drums on the left side, followed by the rest of the drum set, then the bass and the guitars, and ending with the lead vocal on the right, as in the recording of "Easy Street." Laying out the instruments the same way each time speeds up the process, because you start to develop spatial associations with where you expect to find each instrument. The process of reordering tracks is shown in Video Example 3-14.

VIDEO EXAMPLE 3-14. How to reorder tracks.

EXERCISE 3-14: *Reorder the tracks in the reorder.song session.*

The more tracks you have and the more sessions you produce, the more important it becomes to have a system to document your work. Maintain a chronologically organized logbook to preserve such pieces of information as the differences between various versions of projects, what microphones you used, the positions they were placed in, the dates, and the names of people you worked with. Diagramming the setups and taking down measurements will help you re-create arrangements that have produced good results. Include a collection of studio photos or videos. Some of this information can be saved in the song session file itself, such as the title, album, songwriter, genre, year, website, and copyright information. Metadata saved in an MP3 file shows up in some media players and may be of interest to listeners. To access the song information page, click on Studio One > Preferences > Song Setup (Figure 3-9).

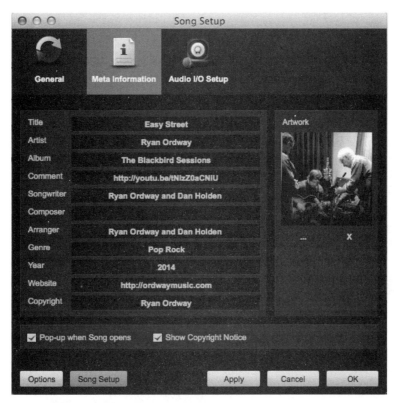

Figure 3-9. The Song Setup window.

Main Outs

Now that we know how to get an optimal layout of the information on the screen, we can create enough space to work on the Main Out. The entire stereo mix goes out through the Main Out channel, and any changes we make to it will affect the entire mix. The Main fader should be set equal to or higher than the individual tracks on the left. If your output exceeds the dynamic limit, you will see a red box appear with the number in it that indicates how many samples clipped. If you invoke the Song > Export Mixdown command at this point, Studio One will warn you as it goes how many dBs out of bounds the mix has gone. If that number becomes large or you hear distortion, you should click on the red box to clear it and turn down the track and bus channel faders a little and try playing back the mix again. The best way to turn down all tracks by the same amount is to group them together before moving one of the faders (Video Example 3-15). This saves you from having to fiddle with changing each fader's position while trying to maintain the same the proportion and disturbing the balance for the tracks you worked so hard to create.

VIDEO EXAMPLE 3-15. Creating a group to use one fader to change the volume of a number of tracks.

EXERCISE 3-15: *Group all the faders in group.song and then turn them up and down as a group.*

We will talk about how to control tone controls in Chapter 5, but you may wish to experiment with inserting the Multiband Dynamics plug-in on the Main Out bus and see if you like the effect it provides as it compresses five individual frequency bands so that no one frequency range sticks out (Video Example 3-16). If you want your song to fade out, you can automate the Main fader.

VIDEO EXAMPLE 3-16. Inserting a multiband compressor and a reverb on the Main output.

EXERCISE 3-16: *Insert a Multiband Dynamics compressor and a reverb on the Main Out.*

Answer quiz questions 3.9–3.13.

REVIEW

In this chapter, we applied techniques introduced in Chapter 2 to find basic levels for the tracks that can then be developed using doubling, panning, and fills to create textures that will engage the listener.

A number of tools like track naming and colors, standard layouts, narrowing tracks, and increasing the size of the Console window can help the engineer deal with the growing amount of information presented as the number of tracks in a session increases.

INTERVIEWS

Two interviews were performed for this chapter; the first, with Ken Scott, appears below. An interview with Ryan Ordway, the composer and singer of "Easy Street," can be found on the book's companion website, lovelythinking.com, where he talks about the experience of recording the song with the master.

Interview with Ken Scott

Ken Scott was 16 years old when he got his first job working at what became Abbey Road Studios in 1964. After working for six months in the tape library, he became second engineer for the Beatles' *A Hard Day's Night* album and was later promoted to record songs on *Magical Mystery Tour* and *The Beatles* (better known as "The White Album"). Since then he has engineered and produced recordings for musicians such as David Bowie, Elton John, Pink Floyd, Supertramp, Mahavishnu Orchestra, Kansas, Dixie Dregs, and Missing Persons.

RW: Do you have any memories of the approach you took recording "Easy Street" or suggestions for what readers might try when they are remixing it?

KS: It was my typical approach: Get the sound in the studio, not the control room, and keep it simple.

RW: Your book *Abbey Road to Ziggy Stardust* provides background on how you mastered your craft, along with interesting stories about other albums and the Epik Drums EDU DVDs. There's so much useful information on how to record and work with drums. Do you have any other suggestions for readers who are just starting to learn how to record and mix?

KS: Firstly, the most important gear in any studio is the monitoring system. If the monitors are true, you can use the cheapest (shittiest) gear in the world and work to get a good sound. If the monitors are hyped, you can be using the best gear in the world and it will turn out sounding awful. There's a story in the book about "Hey Jude" [and how the monitor speakers at the Trident studio had a lot of extra-high frequencies, so that when the musicians later got back to Abbey Road and heard the recording, it sounded like there were pillows across the speakers]. The other thing is: Everything starts in the studio. The sound, the performance—get it right in there, and as an engineer, you have to do very little. Which of course brings me to the last thing: *Keep it simple.* Just because you have 50, 100, or 1,000 plug-ins doesn't mean you have to use them. If it was right in the studio to start with, all you have to do is add a little icing on the cake. The sound needs to start there and the performance should most certainly come from there. I'm not a fan of "we got enough to cut and paste it." That's bullshit. It removes all the humanity and feel. The most important thing is *feel.*

RW: How about when you are mixing?

KS: Keep it simple. I EQ and compress as I record. I like to keep as close to the final mix as possible going throughout the recording process—it's the only way you know what works—and so the final mix, for me, is just that last little bit of tweaking.

RW: You've said that working on four-track machines taught you how to make decisions on the fly, that today there's too much putting off fixing things until the mixing or even mastering stages. What pieces of the puzzle do you have to juggle in your head when you're thinking about what to record on a limited number of tracks? How does making decisions early end up making a better record?

KS: My mindset is the same working with a four-track or with Pro Tools and the seemingly infinite number of tracks that it allows. That mindset is to know what the end result will be. If the end result is not known, you will have no idea what works and what doesn't. Also, try not to get caught up in the minutiae. No record has ever sold, or not sold, because the hi-hat was 1 dB too loud or too quiet in the third verse. Just get the performance.

RW: What is it about the mono mixes of the Beatles reissues that you prefer over the stereo versions? Is it just where the tracks are located in space, or the guarantee of the right balance when everything is combined in one speaker?

KS: I prefer the mono Beatles mixes because up until "The White Album," the band only ever approved the mono mixes. We only ever monitored in mono whilst recording, and so all decisions were made that way. The stereos were just thrown in sometime later and weren't necessarily anything like the previously accepted mono mixes.

RW: How do you decide what projects are worth working on?

KS: Gut. I've worked with acts that I initially thought weren't good, but my gut feeling told me otherwise, and they've turned out to be some of my most successful, and vice versa.

RW: Any advice for music production students?

KS: If you have a plan B, take it. If you can't conceive of doing anything else with your life, you're in the right place, but make sure you enjoy what you do. Enjoyment may be all you get out of it, but that will be worth it.

RYAN ORDWAY: "EASY STREET" CREDITS

Website: ordwaymusic.com
Album title: *The Blackbird Sessions* (Resort Recordings, 2014)
Engineers: Ken Scott assisted by Seth Morton and the Blackbird Academy audio engineering students: Alex Chambers, Sam DeTone, Michael Freeman, Jason Lindsey, Allen Luke, Stephanie Moore, William Newcomb, Dave O'Dell, Tanner Peters, Taylor Pitman, Jake Rabinowitz, Brandon Schnierer, Dillon Stewart, Jeff Todd, Kody Whitehead, Paul Wilson, Logan Witte, Logan Yandell
Studio: Blackbird Studio (Nashville, Tennessee)
Composers: Ryan Ordway and Dan Holden
Musicians: Ryan Ordway, vocal, guitar; Ryan Hommel, acoustic, electric, and pedal steel guitars, background vocals; Dan Holden, keys, background vocals; Marc Seedorf, bass, background vocals; Jeff Armstrong, drums, background vocals

ACTIVITIES

The focus of this chapter is to balance the volume of tracks. That doesn't mean that every track should be equally loud. The challenge is to find the right volume for each track, the volume that puts it in balance with all the others, and to automate changes in volume over the course of the song when needed. Get used to all the parts and what each contributes. Study what is there and look for clues as to what Ken Scott was thinking while he was working—why he decided to double the parts he did, what he recorded, and how the puzzle pieces fit together.

In addition to working with "Easy Street," you may wish to record and mix a song of your own using the techniques covered in this chapter.

Basic

1. Make a mix of "Easy Street" by creating and balancing seven submixes. Open the basic-groups-easy-street.song session file. Create a new folder track in Console view for the drum tracks. Drag each of the seven blue drum tracks into the folder and then change the name of the folder to something meaningful (like "drums"). Create a bus channel for the folder. In the Console view, click on the Banks button and then click on each of the seven drum tracks to hide them, leaving only the submix fader in view. Repeat the process to make folders and submixes for the two brown bass tracks, the three green acoustic guitar tracks, the nine blue

electric guitar tracks, the three violet keyboard tracks, the four green background vocal tracks, and the two orange lead vocal tracks. After doing this, you should have only seven bus channel faders and the main mix in the Console mixer view. Open the folders back up one by one in the Arrange view and work on the individual volume levels for each submix, and then adjust the level of the section with the submix faders in the Console. Take notes on the approach you took. Were there any tracks that you felt should stand out within the folder groups, or did you try to make them blend? Which submixes did you make the loudest, and why? Remember to select the Mute (M) and Solo (S) buttons when you want to hear only certain tracks.

2. Make a list of each instrument's prominence in the verse, chorus, and interlude in "Where You Wanna Be" by Caleb Elliott (Audio Example 3-16), with the loudest instrumental and vocal parts at the top of the list and the softest ones at the bottom. Where do the cellos sit relative to the others? Do you think they are up front enough for an instrumental hook? You'll have an opportunity to mix the song in Chapter 7.

AUDIO EXAMPLE 3-16. "Where You Wanna Be."

3. Find three or more examples of songs of your choosing in different styles where spaces in the lead line are filled by other instruments. List the titles, names of composers, performers, and styles of the songs. Analyze where in the songs the fills are the loudest. Find a recording of at least one other song where there isn't much filling going on. Is some other device being used to provide variety and hold the listener's interest?

Intermediate

1. Open the EasyStreet.song session file. Solo each track to see what is on it and assign all the tracks your own choice of colors. Take notes of what you discover and how you arrived at your color scheme. What is the difference between the 12-string guitar track (egtr 12 str) and the mandolin (oct mando)? When do the second electric tracks come in (egtr2 and egtr2 chamber)? Why does the second of these include "chamber" in the name?

Group the tracks into folders and adjust their relative volumes before closing them and hiding the individual tracks in the Console. Create a bus channel for each folder and find a good balance between the parts. Alternately solo and mute the demo mix track while making notes of ways in which your mix sounds different from it. How do your levels for the acoustic and electric guitars compare? How about your guitar solo? How do the groupings of colors you have compare to the ones chosen by Ken Scott (see orig-tracks-easy-street.song in the EasyStreet folder)? More important than the shades of color, why do you think he grouped them as he did? Challenge: Try making your mix match the demo mix.

2. Record a multitrack session of a song of your own. Give the tracks appropriate names. Use appropriate color coding to suggest the functions and groupings of the tracks. Add markers to indicate the form. Double at least one part. When you mix it, pay special attention to balancing the volume off the tracks.

Advanced

1. Record your own song. Add markers. Set up folders and submixes as needed. Assign colors and names to tracks to help someone else understand how things are organized. Double some parts. Read the parts of the manual about the File > Make New Version and File > Restore Version commands. Make a version in which you limit your panning choices for the tracks to hard left, center, or right, and another version where you have five positions—hard left, left of center, center, right of center, and hard right. Make a written narrative about how you recorded the song, what choices you made in balancing the volume of the tracks, and which panning situation you preferred and why.

2. Remix "Easy Street," incorporating any ideas that occurred to you while doing this chapter's exercises. Experiment with muting some of the doubled parts or making the balance different from the reference mix. Make a version with all the vocals muted, one with no guitar solo, one with the acoustic guitars louder, and another with them softer. Consider rerecording some parts, such as the lead and background vocals, guitar fills, and solo, and changing the instrumental fill. Make greater use of panning to spread some of the tracks out. Export each mix and play the collection on a variety of playback systems. Take notes on what you did to bring some parts out or to blend others together, and any differences you detect in the different situations. Compare and discuss your mixes with those from other people doing the same work.

FOR FURTHER EXPLORATION

+ Ken Scott, *Abbey Road to Ziggy Stardust*. Los Angeles: Alfred Music Publishing, 2012.

+ Ken Scott, Craig Golding, Daniel Rosen, Jay Hodgson, Russ Hepworth-Sawyer, "Interview with Ken Scott." *Journal on the Art of Record Production* 7 (2012).

+ Geoff Emerick, *Here, There, and Everywhere*. New York: Gotham Books, 2007.

+ Wikipedia, "The Beatles' recording technology."

+ Kevin Ryan and Brian Kehew, *Recording the Beatles: The Studio Equipment and Techniques Used to Create Their Classic Albums*. Houston: Curvebender Publishing, 2006. Obsessive documentation of EMI studios and production techniques.

QUIZ QUESTIONS

3.1: Explain the difference between the additive and subtractive approaches to mixing.

3.2: Listen to "Easy Street" (Audio Example 3-17). How well can you hear the piano (i.e., at 0:59, 1:36, 2:50, 3:11)? How about the pedal steel guitar (at 0:08, 0:22, 1:40, 2:08, 2:29)? How do those parts compare with the electric guitar fills at the ends of chorus phrases (at 0:45, 1:46, 2:53) and the guitar solo (at 2:33)? Mixing this song is the focus of this chapter.

AUDIO EXAMPLE 3-17. "Easy Street."

3.3: Did you notice the "Easy Street" background singers? How much do they stick out? How does the level of the lead vocal compare to the background singers?

3.4: Compare the levels of the guitar fills in "Easy Street" (Audio Example 3-17) to those in Adam Ezra's "Sacred Ground" (i.e., at 0:19, 1:25, 1:49, and 2:42 to the end in Audio Example 3-18). Are they about the same or noticeably different? How do the levels of the acoustic guitars in the two songs compare? You'll have an opportunity to mix this song in Chapter 7.

AUDIO EXAMPLE 3-18. "Sacred Ground."

3.5: Listen to how the thickness of the texture of the rhythm guitars changes in Magda's "Stuck In Between" (Audio Example 3-19). How much space is left during the verses for the singer, when she sings in her lower register ("All I ever wanted . . . so the dream was planted"), compared with the choruses ("I can't live this way here without you"), when the melody goes higher? You'll have an opportunity to mix this song in Chapter 7.

AUDIO EXAMPLE 3-19. "Stuck In Between," sung by Magda.

3.6: Listen again to "Easy Street" (Audio Example 3-17). On which words in the lyrics does the lead-vocal double (ld voc comp dbl) start in the EasyStreet.song session?

3.7: What are all the words the background groups of singers (gp bgv 1 and gp bgv 2) sing over the course of the song?

3.8: Where do the low background singers (lo bgv and lo bgv dbl) first appear? You may wish to locate the parts in relation to the markers visible at the top of the Arrange window indicating the order of verses (V) and choruses (Ch).

3.9: Which tracks will have reverb added after doing Exercise 3-16?

3.10: Listen to Audio Example 3-20. How is Audio Example 3-21 different?

AUDIO EXAMPLE 3-20.

AUDIO EXAMPLE 3-21.

3.11: How is Audio Example 3-21 different from Audio Example 3-22?

AUDIO EXAMPLE 3-22.

3.12: How is Audio Example 3-22 different from Audio Example 3-23?

AUDIO EXAMPLE 3-23.

3.13: How is Audio Example 3-23 different from Audio Example 3-24?

AUDIO EXAMPLE 3-24.

STUDIO ONE SHORTCUTS

Toggle loop mode on and off: /
Group selected tracks: Ctrl/Cmd + G
Dissolve group of selected tracks: Ctrl/Cmd + Shift + G

CHAPTER 4

EDITING

GOAL AND OBJECTIVES

After working through this chapter, you will be able to use editing tools to polish recordings.

- Fix rhythm.
- Replace or delete unwanted material.
- Combine the best sections from multiple takes.

PREREQUISITES

- You will need to have Studio One installed and access to the supplemental media to do the exercises in this chapter.
- Understanding the meanings of amplitude and waveform (Chapter 1) will make it easier to use visual editing tools effectively.

THEORY AND PRACTICE

In this chapter we will look at a number of ways that editing can be used to make producing recordings more efficient, such as deleting pauses and extraneous noises, removing or covering up mistakes or profanity, and combining the best parts from repeated attempts. In addition to fixing performances, editing can be used as an arranging tool to construct a song by adding or subtracting sections.

Nondestructive Editing

Emile Berliner invented the Gramophone in the 1890s. A record of the pressure variations in a sound wave was cut directly into a disc from start to end during the process, after which the disc could not be edited.

Magnetophones, the precursors of tape recorders, were invented in the 1930s. Sound was recorded on plastic tape coated with metal particles as it was drawn past a recording head. One of the advantages of this system was that the tape could be edited by cutting it into pieces, which could be reassembled in a new order so that mistakes could be eliminated and the best parts of different recordings combined.

Recording digital audio on hard drives began in the 1980s. Digital recordings are saved in *nonlinear storage*, which means you can jump to any point without having to fast forward or rewind through a tape to find a particular spot in the music. Having instant access to any spot in a digital recording makes recording, playback, and editing go much more quickly.

Today we do our editing with computers. One advantage of digital systems is that they make it possible to do *nondestructive editing*. The user gives the computer instructions about where to start and stop reading audio data out of memory, and then that part of the recording is played back in any order and repeated as many times as desired without changing the original recording. Anytime you make a mistake, you can just use your computer's Undo command, something that is not possible when slicing a piece of analog tape with a razor blade—once you cut the tape, you no longer have the recording of the whole song in one strip, and each piece can be used only once.

Be aware, however, of the risks that come with this wonderful digital technology. For example, it is possible to spend hours editing a song and in the process end up sucking the life out of it by eliminating the natural variations that are part of human performance. Learn as many shortcuts as you can for the editing operations you do most often, and get a vertical mouse, trackball, or other pointing device to minimize your use of a standard mouse—the little moments of tension that take place while pointing, clicking, and dragging add up over time and can cause repetitive stress injuries. Take time to consider the ergonomics of your setup, including the height of your monitor, keyboard, and other peripherals. Remember to take frequent breaks to stretch and change position.

Using Editing Tools to Fix Mistakes

In this chapter you'll learn a number of editing techniques to improve recordings. The first one we'll look at is trimming a ragged start or end of an audio event to get rid of extraneous noises and pauses.

Audio that is recorded in computer programs is usually displayed in boxes running along the horizontal timeline. Studio One calls each box an "audio event" and offers you eight tools for editing them (Figure 4-1). Let's see what each tool is for, starting with the Arrow tool on the left and working our way to the right.

Figure 4-1. Icons for Studio One's editing tools.

Arrow tool (shortcut "1"). Drag events earlier (left) or later (right) in the timeline or vertically between tracks. Each audio event has a *volume envelope* that controls its volume over the course of the event. Click on an audio event with the Arrow tool to display the volume envelope's handles in the upper left and right corners, which you can drag to create a fade-in or fade-out. The overall volume of the entire audio event can be adjusted by clicking on the center of the volume envelope and then dragging the handle up or down.

Range tool (shortcut "2"). Select a range or area by clicking and dragging within an event with the Range tool. Once a range has been selected, it can be deleted by pressing delete.

Split tool (shortcut "3"). Click on part of the waveform with the Split tool to divide single audio events into one or more events that can then be individually edited. The selection point will jump to the nearest grid line if snapping is turned on.

Eraser tool (shortcut "4"). Click on an event to delete it.

Paint tool (shortcut "5"). Create a new track in the Arrange window, add notes to an instrument track, or draw in automation envelopes. Click and hold the button to open a drop-down menu from which different shapes can be selected.

Mute tool (shortcut "6"). Clicking on an individual event with the Mute tool doesn't mute the whole track, just that event.

Bend tool (shortcut "7"). If you have the audio bend option engaged and are showing bend markers, you can use the Bend tool to drag bend markers to new positions on the timeline.

Listen tool (shortcut "8"). Click and hold on any audio event to hear it played alone, starting from the position you click on.

John Glenn was the first American to orbit the Earth in space, and after his return he addressed an audience in New York City. Listen to Audio Example 4-1 and notice the fairly long pause between the words "progress." and "The first two steps." Locate the pause in the waveform in Figure 4-2. Video Example 4-1 shows how to remove it to create a shorter sound bite.

AUDIO EXAMPLE 4-1. The long pause could be edited out.

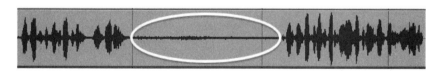

Figure 4-2. Waveform of Audio Example 4-1.

If you are working with music that was recorded with a click track, you may want to perform your edits with the Snap function turned on, so that Studio One will help you find the start of the beat you want to edit. If you have recorded or imported music without a click track, it is easier to work if you turn snapping off. Figure 4-3 shows where the control is located.

Figure 4-3. To turn snapping off, un-highlight the box to the left of Snap.

Video Example 4-1 shows how the pause in Glenn's speech can be selected with the Range tool and then cut out using the delete command. This doesn't work well, however, because it leaves an acoustic hole as seen in Figure 4-4 and heard in Audio Example 4-2.

VIDEO EXAMPLE 4-1. Deleting a selection leaves a gap.

EXERCISE 4-1: *Select and delete the pause in the first-american.song session.*

Figure 4-4. A gap is left in the audio event after deleting a selection.

AUDIO EXAMPLE 4-2. Notice the total silence that remains in the deleted region.

Total silences do not normally occur in the real world. When someone stops talking, there is still some *room noise* in the environment. The completely silent gaps in an edited recording are called *dead air*, and they will signal to listeners that the recording has been manipulated. A better way to do the job would be to select the pause as we did before, but then to use the Delete Time command (Ctrl + Alt + D/Opt + Cmd + D), so that the audio that remains on the right moves over to fill in the gap. Video Example 4-2 demonstrates this process.

VIDEO EXAMPLE 4-2. Deleting time doesn't leave a hole.

EXERCISE 4-2: *Select and delete the pauses in the first-american.song session.*

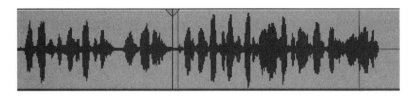

Figure 4-5. Now there is no gap.

AUDIO EXAMPLE 4-3. The edit works much better now, without the dead air.

Sometimes it's possible to hear that an edit has been made, depending on the material and where you cut it. If this happens, you can make a *crossfade* across the edit point—fading out the end of the first region while fading in the beginning of the second region. This technique for smoothing the transitions between edit points is demonstrated in Video Example 4-3.

VIDEO EXAMPLE 4-3. Apply fades between two regions.

EXERCISE 4-3: *Create a crossfade in the crossfade.song session file.*

Answer quiz questions 4.1–4.3, found at the end of the chapter.

Recording music with a click track makes it easier to edit afterward. Video Example 4-4 shows the process of setting up the metronome and recording while listening to the click track and then editing that recording with snapping turned on. Using the Split and Arrow tools with snapping turned on makes it easier delete a measure than dragging with the Range tool. You may find that clicking the mouse button three times is less fatiguing than holding the mouse down while dragging.

VIDEO EXAMPLE 4-4. How to record a series of words while listening to a click track and delete the measures in which the words were spoken off the beat.

EXERCISE 4-4: *Edit out the measures with offbeat words in the offbeat.song session file.*

Many times you don't want to cut out a whole measure. There may just be certain notes that are not right on the beat amid others that are OK. One way to move individual sounds is to separate them with the Split tool and then drag them to the correct places with the Arrow tool. If you trim the sound very close to its start, you can then place the start of the audio event right on the beat. This is demonstrated in Video Example 4-5.

VIDEO EXAMPLE 4-5. Moving the offbeat words, rather than cutting out the measures.

EXERCISE 4-5: *Move the offbeat words in the offbeat.song session to tighten up the rhythm.*

Editing music that was recorded without a click track can take a bit of fussing to get right, since there isn't a grid to snap it to. After you get an audio event roughly in the right position, you can *nudge* it to the right (shortcut Alt/Opt + Right Arrow) or to the left (Alt/Opt + Left Arrow). If Snap is enabled, the event will move by the current snap value; otherwise, nudging movement will be measured by millisecond, as demonstrated in Video Example 4-6.

VIDEO EXAMPLE 4-6. How to nudge events onto the beat.

EXERCISE 4-6: *Record yourself saying, "A, B, C, M, E, F, G, D" without a click track (or use the alphabet.song session), and then edit it to make it "A, B, C, D, E, F, G."*

Answer quiz question 4.4.

Replacing Mistakes

In Video Example 4-1, you saw how to trim the start or end of an audio event by clicking and dragging its boundaries with the Arrow tool. One of the advantages of nondestructive editing is that if you change your mind later and decide you want to get the part back that you trimmed, you can just pull the boundary of the audio event back to where it was. In Exercises 4-1 and 4-2, you removed audio from the middle of an audio event by selecting or splitting it and then deleting it. A third option is to record over the mistake in a process called *overdubbing*.

Studio One offers two recording modes: Overdub and Replace. When you record a track in Overdub mode, what you record gets added to what was already on the track. This could be useful if you were trying to build up a percussion section, for example. Each time through a passage, you could add another instrument and gradually build up a whole rhythm section on just one track. The second option is Replace mode, which allows you to cover up what was previously recorded on the track. This is the method of choice when you want to record over a mistake.

Let's go back to the badly timed words in Exercise 4-4.

Figure 4-6. We need to replace the four badly timed words.

There is usually more than one way to fix a particular editing problem. One would be to duplicate a place where the words were well timed and then to use it to cover the mistakes. This might be the quickest way, but the listener could detect the repetition. Another approach would be to record over the three middle words. In the days of tape recorders, the engineer would rewind the tape to a point a little ways before the section, to give the musicians a chance to hear the part to be replaced in context. The amount of time given to the musicians to orient themselves was called *preroll*. When the tape reached the place where recording was to begin, the engineer would *punch in* the record button to start recording from that point, and then *punch out* at the end to stop recording. This could be a nerve-racking because there was the risk that some of the good material could be accidentally erased.

Punching in with a digital recording system is risk-free. Open the Options menu and select Mode Replace so you will be recording over rather than adding to a track. You can prepare to punch in by choosing a place where you would like to record and clicking on the Preroll icon to the right of the loop length indicators in the transport (shortcut o). The amount of preroll time can be changed after clicking on the Metronome Settings icon to the right of the record button. Press the record button to begin recording. Recording with preroll is useful when you want to pick up a recording from one spot and continue on indefinitely.

Auto Punch allows you to set both the in and the out points and is a better choice when the region you want to fix is in the middle of something that has been previously recorded. Video Example 4-7 demonstrates how Auto Punch can be done, beginning by showing how the Arrow tool changes to a pencil icon when it is positioned over the bar above the timeline. Dragging the pencil across the bar sets the *in* and *out* points, after which the L and R markers can be dragged up or down if necessary to fine-tune them. Auto Punch is then activated by clicking on the icon in the transport bar (shortcut i), underneath the Preroll button. Select the point where you would like to start playback in the timeline ruler and then press the record button. Recording will begin automatically when the *in* point is reached and stop at the *out* point.

VIDEO EXAMPLE 4-7. Punching in to fix a mistake after setting up the Preroll and Auto Punch parameters.

EXERCISE 4-7: *If you have a microphone, punch in to fix the alphabet.song session.*

Studios often have one or more separate booths to isolate the sound of one instrument from another. This makes it possible to fix one musician's mistake later, while leaving the performances on other tracks alone. If good isolation is not achieved between tracks, then mistakes cannot be fixed as easily. Imagine that a drum set is set up next to an acoustic piano, and the piano player plays her part from start to end perfectly, but the drummer makes a mistake at some point that you decide you'd like to change. You can punch in and replace the drum parts wherever you like, but any sound from the original mistakes the drummer made that leaked into the piano mic will still be mixed in with the recording of the piano.

Answer quiz questions 4.5–4.7.

Combining the Best Parts

It's hard to play a song all the way through without making any mistakes. Trying to patch up a few seconds where there is a problem may not work if the part you need to fix is in the middle of a dense section, where sounds are sustained and there's no place to cleanly punch in and out. When mistakes can't be fixed by punching in, musicians may need to record the same song several times to get a good performance. Each time the song is recorded is called a new *take*. The engineer may offer to combine the best of two or more takes to make a finished product, rather than having the musicians try to play it perfectly from start to finish.

Imagine that a band plays a first take mostly well, but messes up the ending, so they decide to record a second take. When they listen back, they agree that the first take is the best of the two up until the ending, and that the ending was played well enough the second time around. Rather than trying a third take, they ask the engineer to replace the ending on Take 1 with the ending from Take 2 (Figure 4-7).

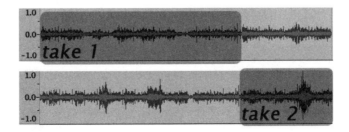

Figure 4-7. Take 1 is the best take of the two up until the end. Take 2 isn't as strong overall, but has a solid ending.

The engineer looks for a place close to the ending to make the switch, in order to keep as much of Take 1 as possible. The final version is a combination of the two.

Figure 4-8. The ending of Take 1 has been replaced with the ending from Take 2.

VIDEO EXAMPLE 4-8. How to edit together parts from two takes.

EXERCISE 4-8: *Open the combine-takes.song session. Edit the ending of Take 2 onto the beginning of Take 1.*

Comping

Sometimes you have a feeling in advance that the best result for a solo would come from combining parts of different takes. In this case, the engineer may have the musician play several passes of the solo and then build a *composite track* by editing the best parts of each. This process is called *comping* a track, for short. See the Studio One manual or the book's companion website for a demonstration of how to use Studio One's "Record Takes to Layers" option to comp a track if you want to try this.

Adding Something New

We started out the chapter by correcting mistakes, either by editing them out or punching in and out to cover them up. Next we learned that you can create a comp track to loop recordings onto a series of layers whose best parts can then be located and consolidated. In this section, we will learn another editing skill: inserting something new at the start or adding something to the end of an existing piece.

Let's return to the speech by John Glenn upon returning from orbiting Earth. You've removed the mayor's fine introduction, cut out the pauses, and may have even taken out references to New York during the speech. Your next task is to add an introduction that provides the context that was eliminated (similar to Audio Example 4-4), and an outro (similar to Audio Example 4-5) at the end to wrap up the segment.

AUDIO EXAMPLE 4-4. Use this intro for Exercise 4-9 if you don't have a microphone.

AUDIO EXAMPLE 4-5. A possible outro for Exercise 4-9.

VIDEO EXAMPLE 4-9. How to add an intro and outro to an existing recording.

EXERCISE 4-9: *Add a recording of yourself making an introduction and ending to the edited version of John Glenn's speech.*

Answer quiz question 4.8.

Creating a New Arrangement

Editing techniques can be used to build arrangements by cutting, extending, or repeating sections to make multiple versions with different lengths from a single recording. Many styles lend themselves to being restructured in this way. In the days before the consolidation of ownership of radio stations, different versions of songs could be heard: three- to four-minute versions on AM and five- to seven-minute versions on FM. Even longer versions could be released for discos, to give patrons more time to find a partner and strut their stuff. The standard cut, copy, and paste shortcuts that are used in most computer programs will work in Studio One, which in addition has its own Duplicate (shortcut d) command.

VIDEO EXAMPLE 4-10. Copying, pasting, and duplicating audio events.

EXERCISE 4-10: *Create echo and stutter effects on a recording of yourself saying "Hello."*

Answer quiz question 4.9.

Fixing Rhythm

Another type of editing involves adjusting the start times of events so that they are played closer to the beat. Engineers most often do this when editing rhythm section parts such as the drums and bass. There are a few tricks to make such micro-editing more efficient, which will save time and won't tire out your hand and arm so much. As you evaluate the ergonomics of your workstation, this might be a good time to consider purchasing a trackball, vertical mouse, or other pointing device to reduce the amount of clicking and dragging you have to do.

Other ways to reduce the strain on your arm are to learn as many keyboard shortcuts as you can and take breaks. Even better, find musicians who can play parts accurately so that there is less editing to be done. If you're playing the parts yourself, it may be faster, be more enjoyable, and end up sounding better if you practice a part before recording it, rather than recording it sloppily and then having to spend hours trying to edit it into shape.

A *metronome* is a device that produces a series of clicks that musicians use to practice and record at a steady tempo. In a recording studio, the metronome click tracks are played through headphones instead of loudspeakers, so that the sound won't be picked up by microphones. When the musicians and computer agree on the tempo defined by the metronome, it becomes possible later to snap and *quantize*, a process that automatically moves selected events to the nearest beat subdivisions defined by the Arrangement grid. The grid is marked by the ticks in the timeline. To extend vertical lines from those ticks down through the background of the Arrangement window, go to Studio One > Preferences > Advanced and select the option to allow grid lines to shine through.

The grid uses the Timebase settings (located above the Snap button) as the basis for its display. When working with a metronome, you should set the Timebase to Bars, which will display time in bars and beats. If you don't record with a metronome, then the time division grid on the screen has no relationship to what the musicians are playing, which limits the options the engineer later has for editing.

Simple metronomes that just click once per beat can be hard to play along with, as they get covered up by what the musicians are playing. More sophisticated models allow the engineers to set one or more subdivisions between the beats, but these are often still not very inspiring to play with, due to the tones used. You may wish to record while listening to the drum loops that come with your recording software instead of a click track, and then later go back and remove the loops if they aren't appropriate for the finished product.

The best type of click track may be the one you make yourself, as Tony Daigle did for the musicians recording "Where You Wanna Be" (Chapter 7). Even simple drum loops can be easier and more fun to play along with than the built-in metronome. If you turn on snapping and set the beat subdivision, you can drag a kick drum, snare drum, and hi-hat cymbal onto a track at the appropriate times to create a basic beat. Figures 4-9 and 4-10 show how music notation can be converted to a Studio One track. Compare the built-in metronome sound in Audio Example 4-6 with this fabricated version (Audio Example 4-7). Be sure to experiment with the options for native sounds if you do use Studio One's built-in metronome.

Figure 4-9. Music notation for a basic rock beat.

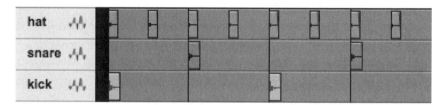

Figure 4-10. The same beat transferred to the corresponding subdivisions in three Instrument tracks in Studio One.

AUDIO EXAMPLE 4-6. A 4/4 bar marked by the built-in metronome.

AUDIO EXAMPLE 4-7. One bar of the homemade drumbeat.

Once you've created a one- or two-measure beat, you can select and Duplicate ("d") it as many times as you wish (Figure 4-11, Audio Example 4-8).

Figure 4-11. The one-bar drumbeat turned into an eight-bar section.

AUDIO EXAMPLE 4-8. Eight bars of 4/4.

VIDEO EXAMPLE 4-11. How to create a drum pattern to use in place of a click track.

EXERCISE 4-11: *Create an eight-bar drumbeat using the provided kick.wav, snare.wav, and hihat. wav samples provided.*

AUDIO EXAMPLE 4-9. Kick drum sample.

AUDIO EXAMPLE 4-10. Snare drum sample.

AUDIO EXAMPLE 4-11. Hi-hat cymbal sample.

Answer quiz questions 4.10 and 4.11.

It would be tedious and tiring to fix up a track by hand when there are many notes whose timing is off. Fortunately, there are tools that can go a long way toward automating the process. It is easiest to take advantage of these if the musicians record their parts while listening to a click track.

In addition to setting up a metronome so that the musicians and computer are in agreement as to where the beats are, the engineer must decide how finely to divide up the time grid horizontally in order to automate the process of improving timing. Check the "Introduction to Music Notation" page at lovelythinking.com if you'd like to understand how rhythms are written and how they correspond to the timing grid in Studio One.

Listen to the performance in Audio Example 4-12 of a musician whose timing was off. The performer was listening to a metronome while recording, but made a couple of obvious timing mistakes in the second measure. This lack of precision can be seen in Figure 4-12.

AUDIO EXAMPLE 4-12. Ragged quarter notes.

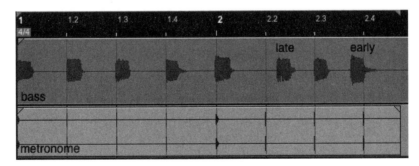

Figure 4-12. The timing of the notes as played.

Look at Figure 4-12 to see what was played, paying special attention to how the timing of the notes lines up with the time grid based on the quarter-note quantization settings in effect. Notice that one note is late (to the right of a grid line) and another is early (to the left of a grid line). There will always be some amount of difference between what a metronome and a human play. Slight discrepancies contribute to the feel of the music and are not mistakes.

The start times of the notes have to be located before they can be individually aligned to the beat. This could be done manually, as you did in Exercise 4-5 with the Split tool, but the computer can do it automatically by taking advantage of the presence of high-frequency *transients* that signal the beginnings of notes. If you want Studio One to help fix the timing of the notes, you can open the Bend panel by clicking on the Audio Bend icon. Clicking on the Analyze button creates bend markers at the start of each note (Figure 4-13).

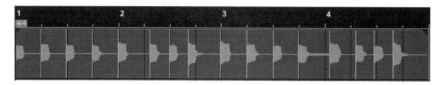

Figure 4-13. Bend markers now appear at beginning of each note.

After the bend markers have been created, we can quantize the notes to make them line up with the grid lines. Click on the Inspector icon above the track column and set the Timestretch mode to Audio Bend for this type of audio material, leave strength set at 100 percent, select quarter-note subdivision for Quantize time grid, and then click on Apply to move each note all the way to the nearest beat, as shown in Figure 4-14 and heard in Audio Example 4-13.

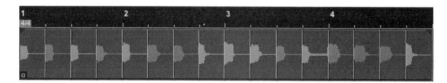

Figure 4-14. Notice how they are all exactly on the beat now.

AUDIO EXAMPLE 4-13. Quantized quarter notes.

The process of correcting the timing of the quarter notes is demonstrated in Video Example 4-12.

VIDEO EXAMPLE 4-12. How to quantize audio using bend markers.

EXERCISE 4-12: *Quantize the audio in ragged-quarters.song.*

Quantizing with a strength of 100 percent makes the rhythm mechanical, as if the part were played by a machine. This can be desirable in styles like electronic dance music, but it could suck the life out of the swing feel in jazz. When quantizing with a strength of 50 percent, the start time of each note moves halfway toward the nearest quantization subdivision. This tightens up the rhythm while still leaving a human quality. The same performance by the bass player quantized by 50 percent is shown in Figure 4-15 and heard in Audio Example 4-14. This has helped, but to really fix this performance, a stronger quantization setting would be needed, since the mistakes are so far off the beat.

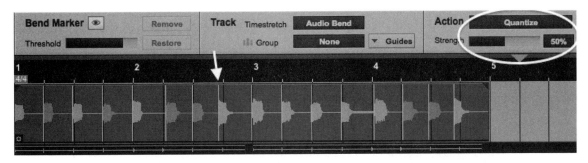

Figure 4-15. When quantized with a strength of 50 percent, notes are nudged halfway to the nearest grid line.

AUDIO EXAMPLE 4-14. The bass notes quantized with a strength of 50 percent.

VIDEO EXAMPLE 4-13. Changing the quantization strength.

EXERCISE 4-13: *Experiment with quantizing the bass notes between 50 and 100 percent in ragged-quarters.song.*

We chose a quantization grid before of quarter notes because that was the shortest note the bass player played. There are shorter and longer note durations. Figure 4-16 shows how the quantization level corresponds to the note values being played.

Figure 4-16. Quantization levels are based on note values such as quarter, eighth, or sixteenth notes.

Now let's ask the bass player to record a new combination of quarter and eighth notes (Figure 4-17, Audio Example 4-15).

Figure 4-17. Musical notation of two bars of quarter and eighth notes.

AUDIO EXAMPLE 4-15. The bass player's attempt at this new challenge.

Our grid will not be finely enough spaced for this passage if we stick with the quarter-note quantization grid setting. Quantizing the notes in the first measure will work fine, since they are all quarter notes, but when we get to the second measure, the eighth notes that lie between the quarter-note clicks of the metronome will not be quantized correctly. The rule to remember is that whenever you quantize, you should pick a grid setting that is equal to or smaller than the value of the shortest notes played. Since the last musical example included eighth notes, we need to change the grid to eighth notes (Figure 4-18).

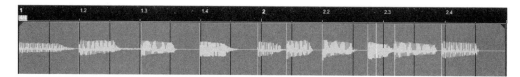

Figure 4-18. The quantization grid set to eighth notes.

After changing the spacing of the grid lines, we can quantize the second measure and correct the eighth-note motion (Figure 4-19, Audio Example 4-16).

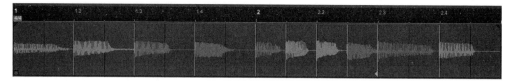

Figure 4-19. Quantizing with an eighth-note grid base setting moves the notes correctly to the nearest eighth note.

AUDIO EXAMPLE 4-16. The eighth notes in the second measure are now time-corrected.

The process of changing the quantization grid is demonstrated in Video Example 4-14.

VIDEO EXAMPLE 4-14. Changing the quantization grid from quarter to eighth notes.

EXERCISE 4-14: *Compare the quantization of the bass notes with grid lines at quarter and eighth notes using the 8-and-4-notes.song session.*

Answer quiz questions 4.12–4.14.

Manipulating Pitch

In addition to quantizing the timing of notes, Studio One provides two tools to move the pitch of notes. Select an audio event and then click on the Inspector icon and change the Transpose value to move up or down to a new key, or make finer adjustments in the Tune box.

Celemony's auto tuning program Melodyne is integrated into Studio One and makes it easier to change the pitch of individual notes. If you have the Professional version, you can type Ctrl/Cmd + M and experiment with it to see if auto-tuning is something you are interested in using. Consult the *Studio One Reference Manual* and Celemony's website for more information. Two ways of changing the pitch of notes are shown in Video Example 4-15.

VIDEO EXAMPLE 4-15. Two ways of changing the pitch of notes.

EXERCISE 4-15: *Try improving the pitch in the out-of-tune.song session file.*

REVIEW

In this chapter we've covered a variety of techniques to improve upon recordings, including fixing the timing of events by moving them by hand or automatically, using quantization. We've replaced and deleted pauses and mistakes, and combined the best parts of different takes to make the best composite track. This will allow you to polish your recordings and make them sound more professional. Keep your eyes and ears open for opportunities to use the same techniques for creative purposes by making new arrangements out of blocks of sound.

It's worth memorizing the editing tool shortcuts and editing techniques introduced in this chapter, as they will really help speed up your workflow and reduce the amount of repetitive movements you would otherwise have to perform with the mouse.

ACTIVITIES

The following activities will give you a chance to use the editing techniques presented in this chapter to fix mistakes and add new musical elements. Think about recordings you may have in your collection that you could edit in a variety of ways.

Basic

1. Find an audio recording of a short speech on the Internet and edit out the pauses and less critical phrases, as you did with John Glenn's speech in Exercise 4-2.

2. Open the motherless-child-unquantized.song session and quantize the bass and piano parts.

Intermediate

1. Find an audio recording of a short speech on the Internet or record someone speaking, and then insert your own introduction and tag on an ending, as you did with the edited version of John Glenn's speech in Exercise 4-9.

2. Find a recording of a speech and bleep out certain words to create a comic effect, as if the person had been cursing. Paste the supplied 1,000 Hz beep (Audio Example 4-17) in places over the original recording.

AUDIO EXAMPLE 4-17. A beep to bleep with.

Advanced

1. Take a speech of your choosing and synchronize the words with the rhythm of a song. Analyze the voice track for transients and then quantize the words to fit the beat subdivisions or a groove template.

2. Create a rhythm track for a chord progression you have in mind, as you did in Exercise 4-11. Record a track with a chord progression while listening to it, and then quantize it to tighten the rhythm. Record a second track with a solo over it. Punch in a section of the solo that you think could be improved. Mute the second track and create a third track for a new solo. Comp the new solo by recording layers and then assemble the best sections. Listen back to each of the two resulting solos one at a time. How do they compare? Create a fourth track and see if you can top what you've done so far.

FOR FURTHER EXPLORATION

Some possibilities sources for public domain recordings are listed on the book's companion website at lovelythinking.com.

Read from the *Studio One Reference Manual*:

+ Chapter 6 on editing
+ The sections on Metronome Control and Loop Recording from the chapter on recording

QUIZ QUESTIONS

4.1: How can you tell if snapping mode is turned on?

4.2: Explain under what circumstances you'd want to turn snapping mode on.

4.3: How would the process of editing John Glenn's speech be affected if snapping mode was turned on? Make a drawing as part of your answer.

4.4: What determines the horizontal spacing of the vertical lines that events snap to when snapping is turned on?

4.5: What are punching in and punching out? What are they used for?

4.6: What do in and out points represent? How are they set?

4.7: What is preroll? Describe a situation in which you might want to use it.

4.8: Describe the steps you would go through to produce a short program combining previously recorded material with a new introduction and ending.

4.9: Describe a situation in which the Duplicate command would be a better choice than copying and pasting.

4.10: Why is it important to record with the metronome or click track on if you plan on editing the timing of a track?

4.11: What would you have to do if you wanted to adjust the timing of a track of hand claps to line up with what the rest of the band played, if you didn't have a metronome or click track?

4.12: What are transients?

4.13: Where do transients usually appear when the sound's waveform is displayed?

4.14: How do transients help make the editing process more efficient?

Answers to the quiz questions can be found in Appendix C.

STUDIO ONE SHORTCUTS

KEY COMMAND	RESULT
1	Select Arrow tool
2	Select Range tool
3	Select Split tool
4	Select Eraser tool
6	Select Mute tool
8	Select Listen
i	Turn on Auto Punch
O	Turn on
Ctrl	Bounce
Ctrl/	Undo
d	Duplicate
t	New track
Tab	Move from one set of transients to the next
Alt/Opt + Right Arrow	Nudge right
Alt/Opt + Left Arrow	Nudge left

TONE

GOAL AND OBJECTIVES

After working through this chapter, you should be able to choose an appropriate filter to affect a sound in the desired way.

+ Apply a variety of filters to modify tone.
+ Explain what frequency is, and how complex sounds are made of sine wave components.
+ Demonstrate what the graph of a spectrum represents.

PREREQUISITES

+ Chapter 1: Understand frequency and hertz (Hz).
+ Chapter 2: Understand amplitude, dB, and waveform.

THEORY AND PRACTICE

The information presented in this chapter will help you understand what tone is and start to develop techniques to control it. This chapter is the longest and most theory-heavy in the book because tone is such an important part of the music production process and something that is new to most people. Of the main mixing tasks of volume balancing, tone control, and editing, tone is the least familiar. While many of our audio devices offer the user control over volume, few provide the same opportunities to make changes in tone. While we may not have much experience with editing audio, we have at least had some experience inserting, copying, pasting, and deleting text.

Tone control is one of the most challenging and creative aspects of mixing. In addition to fixing problems in recordings, it can be used to create special effects that help focus the listener's attention. Like a painter who has mastered how to combine different shades of color, an experienced engineer can use tone to separate or blend sound elements in a mix.

What Is Tone?

Tone (or *timbre* in French) is the quality of sound that is left when you take away its pitch and loudness. The tone of a particular voice helps you pick it out in a crowd and tell how a speaker is feeling. The closer you get to the speaker, the clearer the tone of their voice becomes, providing a sense of intimacy. Over time, as you listen and observe musicians, you learn to identify the instruments they play by the tones they produce. Many instruments can play middle C, but each one plays it with a different tone.

In Audio Example 5-1, three instruments take turns playing the same pitch. What differentiates instruments is tone and how it changes over time.

AUDIO EXAMPLE 5-1. Flute, piano, and accordion.

As your experience grows, you may become aware of the variations in tone among different models of the same type of instrument—for example, different brands of acoustic guitars, which are affected by the types of wood used, the construction design, and gauge and age of strings.

Words Fail

Languages evolve to suit the needs of the people who use them. The Inuit-Yupik peoples in Alaska have many words to describe different types of snow and ice. The Sami in northern parts of Scandinavia and Russia may have as many as 1,000 words for types of reindeer, words that would have no counterpart in a language spoken in a tropical climate where snow and reindeer don't exist. While school children get by with the primary colors in their set of crayons, painters learn to identify a wide range of shades. There are more than 16 million different color combinations available on the Internet that can be achieved by combining different amounts of red, green, and blue light.

Consumers who know how to adjust the bass and treble controls on their stereo systems may not be able to explain what tone is. Musicians and their teachers work intuitively with it to shape their sound, and use words like warm, dull, brittle, clear, breathy, and bright to describe it, but the controls that go into modifying tone are often subtle or internal and therefore invisible to listeners. Audio engineers are the ones ultimately responsible for tone in music production and have the richest vocabulary, including descriptions like boomy, muddy, tubby, thick, hollow, dirty, edgy, and tinny.

EXERCISE 5-1: *Listen to Audio Example 5.1 again and write down your observations regarding the differences in tone between the three instruments.*

AUDIO EXAMPLE 5-1. Flute, piano, and accordion.

The problem with using words to describe tone is that they are not precise enough to describe it and mean different things to different people. When we say, "Don't use that tone of voice with me!" we probably couldn't explain exactly what that tone of voice is. There's no common vocabulary that everyone shares. We need an objective language if we want to communicate with other engineers or machines.

Spectra: Science to the Rescue

As we saw in Chapter 2, expressing a sound's amplitude in units of dB is more precise than using a musician's relative terms of *piano* (soft) and *forte* (loud). The science of acoustics provides the mathematical precision to help us understand tone, as well. Computer recording systems can analyze the tone of a sound and display it graphically, and provide processing tools that engineers can apply in response to what they are hearing and seeing on the screen.

The sounds we hear in the world are a complex combination of different vibration patterns. Sound starts out as a pressure wave sent out from a vibrating object that causes air molecules to be pushed together and pulled apart as the wave passes through them. A waveform is a graph of the change in air pressure of air molecules in a particular place over time. Figure 5-1 shows the waveform of this simple vibration pattern, called a *sine wave*. This is the same pattern that a weight on a spring traces in space over time.

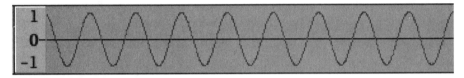

Figure 5-1. The sine wave pattern.

VIDEO EXAMPLE 5-1. Seeing an animation makes it easier to understand that the horizontal axis represents the passage of time.

VIDEO EXAMPLE 5-2. Using PreSonus's Tone Generator plug-in.

EXERCISE 5-2: *Experiment with the Tone Generator plug-in using the tone-generator.song session.*

The sine wave pattern describes the back-and-forth pattern of vibration and is the basic building block of all sounds. The Periodic Table lists more than 100 different chemical elements that go into making matter. In sound there is only one element—the sine wave. The complexity in audio waveforms stems from the fact that air molecules can vibrate at different rates simultaneously.

Vibrating objects, too, can have multiple modes of movement. When you pluck a string, the *fundamental* vibration mode is for the entire string to move back and forth with the middle of the string moving the most. Meanwhile, the two halves also each vibrate back and forth. Shorter things vibrate more quickly than longer ones. If the length of a string is cut in half, its frequency doubles. In musical terms, we would say that the pitch goes up an octave. Figure 5-2 shows the waveforms of the pressure waves created by the whole string vibrating at the fundamental frequency (F0) and the two halves of the string vibrating at two times the fundamental frequency.

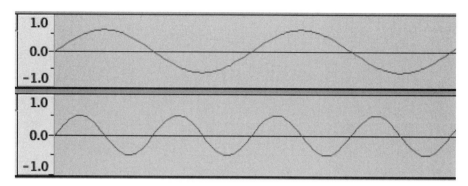

Figure 5-2. The fundamental frequency (top) and the first harmonic (bottom).

The string is doing more than that, however. It is also vibrating in thirds, and fourths, and fifths, and so on. Vibration components that are integer (counting number) multiples like these of the fundamental frequency are called *harmonics*, like two times the fundamental frequency or three times the fundamental. The higher-frequency components usually have lower amplitudes than the fundamental. The more energy there is in the higher-frequency components, the brighter the sound will seem to the listener.

Imagine two hands reaching into a swimming pool and moving at two different vibration rates, one twice as fast as the other. The two individual waves start out as a simple sine wave shape and then where they meet, they mix together to form a more complex wave shape. It is the same with sound wave components. The fundamental frequency and the overtones in a sound start out as sine waves and mix together to form a complex waveform. Looking at the waveform in Figure 5-3, you might be able to pick out the influence of the higher-frequency component as it rides on top of the lower-frequency component, just as you might be able to hear the two sine waves being played together when listening to Audio Example 5-2.

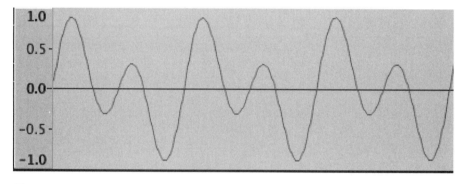

Figure 5-3. The combination of 440 Hz and 880 Hz sine waves.

AUDIO EXAMPLE 5-2. At the beginning only the 440 Hz is playing, and then the 880 Hz is faded in.

Figure 5-4 shows the waveforms of a different fundamental and its first three harmonic overtones. Each component is a sine wave of a different frequency. The components are played one at a time in Audio Example 5-3 and then together in Audio Example 5-4. Harmonic components fuse together and are perceived by the listener as a single note. Figure 5-5 shows the complex waveform that results from adding these waveforms together.

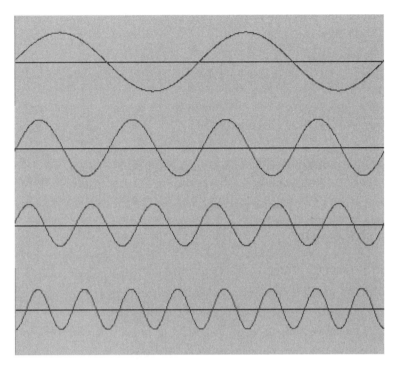

Figure 5-4. Four separate sine wave components.

AUDIO EXAMPLE 5-3. The four sine waves played one at a time.

AUDIO EXAMPLE 5-4. The four components brought in one at a time.

It is now much harder to determine the frequencies of the component waves just by looking at the combined waveform in Figure 5-5, and to pick them out when the combination is played in a typical balance in which the higher harmonics have lower amplitudes (Audio Example 5-5).

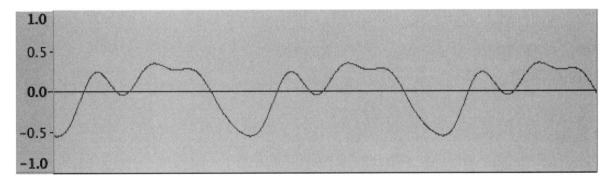

Figure 5-5. Four sine waves added together.

AUDIO EXAMPLE 5-5. One note formed by four sine wave components played all together.

Video Example 5-3 shows eight harmonic components that fuse together to make a single note. Changing the relative volumes of the components changes the tone.

VIDEO EXAMPLE 5-3. Changing the level of the components affects the tone.

EXERCISE 5-3: *Manipulate tone by changing the levels of the faders in the 8-components.song session file.*

The graph of a complex waveform can be helpful when editing a track because it shows where the loud and soft spots are, but is not much use in determining the amplitudes and frequencies of the sine wave components that make up a sound, which is what we need if we are interested in understanding tone. Fortunately, there is another graphical tool designed for this.

Graphing Spectrum

A graph of a sound's *spectrum* (plural *spectra*) shows the frequency and amplitude of the sine wave components it is made from. In the graph of a spectrum, the vertical axis represents amplitude, as it does in the graph of a waveform. The horizontal graph in a waveform graph represents time, but in the spectrum graph it represents frequency. The horizontal position of each vertical line indicates the frequency of that component, and the height of the line is proportional to that sine wave's amplitude. Higher-frequency (treble) components are on the right, and lower-frequency (bass) components are on the left. Babies start out able to hear frequencies from approximately 20 Hz to 20 kHz. Later in life, people often lose some sensitivity in their upper range, depending on their genes, age, and exposure to noise.

Let's go back to the sound we generated using our four-component synthesizer shown in Figure 5-5. The fundamental frequency (F0) of this sound is a sine wave at 130 Hz. Figure 5-6 shows a spectrum of just that first component.

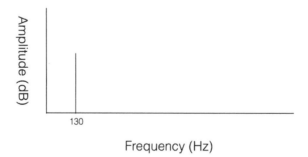

Figure 5-6. The fundamental frequency is the lowest-pitched component.

AUDIO EXAMPLE 5-6. A sine wave at 130 Hz.

Let's add the next component, a harmonic of the fundamental frequency located at 2xF0, or 260 Hz. The amplitude of each higher component is a little less than the lower ones. Now we have two lines on our spectrum graph: the fundamental at 130 Hz, and the first overtone at 260 Hz:

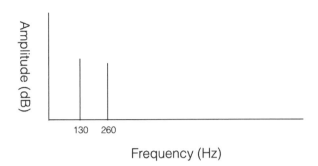

Figure 5-7. The fundamental frequency and first overtone. Compare with its waveform shown in Figure 5-3.

AUDIO EXAMPLE 5-7. Sine waves at 130 Hz and 260 Hz.

Let's add two more components: 3xF0 (390 Hz) and 4xF0 (520 Hz):

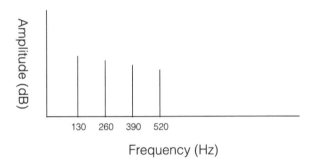

Figure 5-8. F0, F1, F2, and F3.

AUDIO EXAMPLE 5-8. Sine waves at 130 Hz, 260 Hz, 390 Hz, and 520 Hz.

Finally, let's add the last four components: 5xF0 (650 Hz), 6xF0 (780 Hz), 7xF0 (910 Hz), and 8xF0 (1040 Hz), seen in Figure 5-9 and heard in Audio Example 5-9:

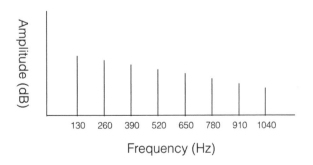

Figure 5-9. F0, F1, F2, F3, F4, F5, F6, and F7.

AUDIO EXAMPLE 5-9. The sum of sine waves at 130 Hz, 260 Hz, 390 Hz, 520 Hz, 650 Hz, 780 Hz, 910 Hz, and 1040 Hz.

The heights of the lines in the spectrum correspond to the positions of faders used to control the amplitude of the various sine wave components in Exercise 5-3, where each fader controls the amplitude of a sine wave at a different frequency (Figure 5-10).

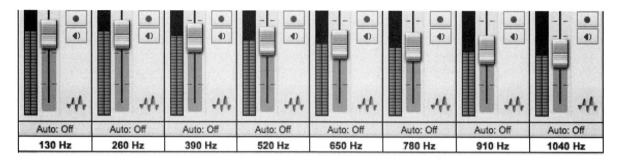

Figure 5-10. The positions of the faders playing sine waves in Studio One control the amplitude of each component in the spectrum.

The relative proportion of amplitudes of the sine wave components is what creates the experience of tone, like the relative strengths of different frequencies of light and concentrations of chemicals provoke sensations of color, taste, and smell. If we increase the amplitude of the upper frequencies, the sound will become brighter (Audio Example 5-10). This will show up in the graph in Figure 5-11 of the spectrum, where the height of the lines representing the higher components is increased.

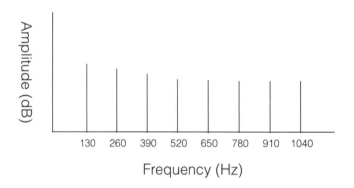

Figure 5-11. The amplitude of the higher components has been increased relative to Figure 5-9.

AUDIO EXAMPLE 5-10. This sound is brighter than the corresponding tone in Audio Example 5-9.

Likewise, if we reduce the amplitude of the higher (treble) components (Figure 5-12) and increase the amplitude of the lower (bass) frequencies, the sound will get darker (Audio Example 5-11).

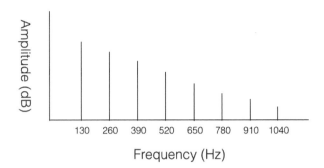

Figure 5-12. The higher treble frequencies have been decreased and the lower bass frequencies increased.

AUDIO EXAMPLE 5-11. This tone has more bass frequencies.

Answer quiz question 5.1, found at the end of this chapter.

A spectrum analyzer doesn't show the same neat single lines as in our idealized spectrum. Instead, each component is represented a little wider, depending on the size of the FFT window being used for analysis. Figure 5-13 shows how Audio Example 5-11 looks in Studio One's Spectrum Meter when using the maximum size. More often you won't need that much precision, and may choose to connect the points with a curve (Figure 5-14).

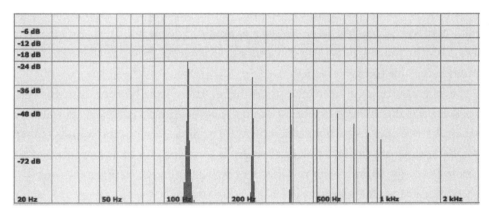

Figure 5-13. Size of FFT window set to 65536.

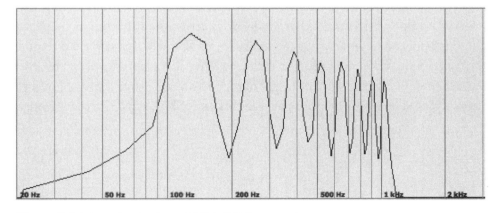

Figure 5-14. Lowering the size to 2048 in FFT Curve mode.

Human beings are designed to notice change. Sounds with steady spectra are not as interesting as those that evolve over time. Short-lived transient frequencies create rapid changes in the spectrum at the beginning of a note and provide the listener with clues about the type of instrument being played. Over the course of a note, the relative amplitudes of the individual components change. The higher components usually get proportionately stronger as the musician plays more loudly. Try imagining the changes in tone you hear when a trumpet is played loudly compared with when it is soft. A spectral analyzer shows how the spectrum of the music changes over time.

VIDEO EXAMPLE 5-4. Each vowel sound has a different spectrum.

EXERCISE 5-4: *Set up a microphone and record yourself slowly repeating, "Shay, fee, sigh, toe, moo." Observe the changes in the spectrum using the Spectrum Meter.*

Answer quiz questions 5.2–5.5.

Effects of Microphones on Tone

The best way to get great tone is to have performers produce it from the start, and have the right microphone in a good place. It is easier to use tone controls to improve upon a good sound than to try to rescue a bad one. As they've been saying for hundreds of years, "You can't make a silk purse out of a sow's ear." The process of getting good tone starts with a musician having a well-maintained instrument and being able to play it well.

When recording electric and electronic instruments, there may be tone controls that affect the sound before it reaches the microphone or input on the audio interface. Electric guitarists can modify the tone of their instruments with knobs that adjust the balance between the sounds from the pickups closer and farther away from the instrument's bridge. The controls on their amplifiers offer additional opportunities to shape the sound. Even the choice of strings and pick changes the sound.

Experienced musicians who listen well to each other often choose to stay out of each other's way by not playing in the same pitch range as another member of the group. This makes it easier for the engineer to get a well-defined mix without a lot of muddiness caused by overlapping frequencies.

Each model of microphone has a characteristic response to sound. The *frequency response* of a device tells you how well it responds to the different frequencies across the spectrum. A frequency response graph for a microphone can be created by recording a series of sine waves at various frequencies, each with the same amplitude. The amplitude that each frequency was picked up at by the microphone is then graphed, as shown in Figure 5-15. The height of each arrow represents the signal strength at which its frequency was picked up by the microphone—in this case, Shure's SM57 dynamic microphone.

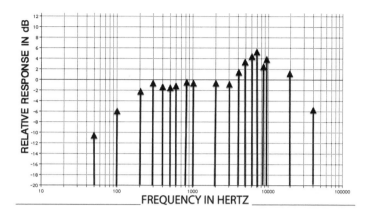

Figure 5-15. The frequency response of an SM57 microphone showing how strongly individual frequencies are picked up.

The tops of the arrows can then be connected with a smooth line as shown in Figure 5-16. From the graph we can see that this microphone, like many dynamic microphones, boosts frequencies around 6 kHz. It does not pick up as well below 100 Hz or above 10 kHz. The bump in the 6 kHz range can be a desirable thing, adding brilliance to voices and brass instruments that are recorded with it.

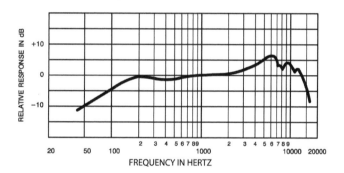

Figure 5-16. The SM57's frequency response, shown as a curved line.

Microphones like the Shure SM57 act as filters by boosting or cutting certain frequencies. Figure 5-17 shows the frequency response of the RØDE NT1 microphone, which shows a *flat* response from the low end and extending on above 10 kHz. The flatness of the line across the frequencies that humans can hear implies that there won't be a lot of loss or boosting of a particular frequency band. This is what is meant when it's said that these microphones are more accurate, making them a popular choice in recording studios.

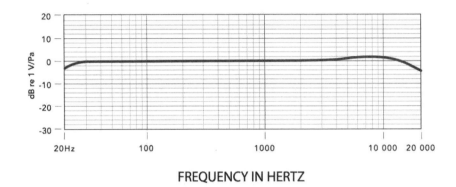

FREQUENCY IN HERTZ

Figure 5-17. The frequency response of a RØDE NT1 microphone, which was used to record the acoustic guitar and electric piano in the next examples.

Modifying Tone with Filters

When two instruments play in the same frequency range, the louder one will tend to cover up the softer, to the point where the softer one is no longer heard. In Figure 5-18 we see a soundstage plot showing an acoustic guitar playing in the center between the two speakers. The left to right position shows where the sound of the guitar is coming from in space. The width of the oval is proportional to its volume, and its height represents its predominant frequency range. Even though it is playing at a low volume, it still comes through clearly in Audio Example 5-12.

AUDIO EXAMPLE 5-12. A guitar in the center of the mix.

An electric piano now added playing a similar rhythm in the same location and frequency range will *mask* or mostly cover up the guitar part, as seen in Figure 5-19 and heard in Audio Example 5-13.

AUDIO EXAMPLE 5-13. The piano masks the guitar.

The engineer has a couple of options to make the sound of both instruments distinct. The first would be to pan the instruments to different sides in the stereo field, to give each instrument a horizontal space in which to be heard, as seen in Figure 5-20 and heard in Audio Example 5-14.

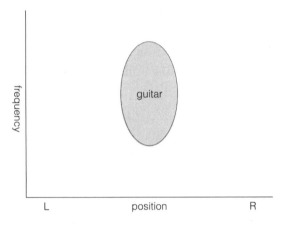

Figure 5-18. A soundstage plot showing the position of a guitar in a stereo mix.

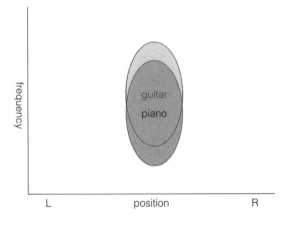

Figure 5-19. A soundstage plot showing how the electric piano obscures the guitar. Both instruments are playing in the same frequency range in the same location in the stereo space.

AUDIO EXAMPLE 5-14. Panning the two instruments apart makes them come through more clearly.

A second option would be to use an *equalizer* (or EQ for short) to control the spectrum of each track, to carve out a space in the spectrum for each instrument. Equalizers contain *filters*—electronic circuits or computer processes that modify the tone of the signals that pass through them. Filters in computer-based recording systems are packaged in *plug-ins*, small software programs that are inserted into the signal. Each EQ plug-in offers different control options. The understanding that we've built up through the discussion of spectra should help us understand how plug-ins affect sounds.

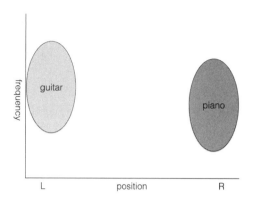

Figure 5-20. A soundstage plot showing the electric piano and guitar separated in space.

Equalization can be accomplished by boosting the frequencies one wants to hear more of, or by cutting those one wishes to hear less of. Subtractive EQ is like sculpture, where the parts of a block of rock that don't belong are chipped away. A variety of filter tools are used in music production, each with a different shape to cut into the spectrum. Many engineers prefer to cut out parts that are getting in the way, rather than boosting parts to make them stand out. It is tempting to boost parts because that raises the overall level of the track, and things usually sound better to us when they get louder. On the other hand, a cleaner, better-defined mix can often be obtained by cutting out parts on competing tracks. You should try both approaches.

The spectrum of the acoustic guitar we've been working with is shown in Figure 5-21. It has most of its energy from 100 Hz to 2 kHz. The electric piano has most of its energy from 40 Hz to 1 kHz (Figure 5-22). Most of the overlap between them is in the 100 Hz to 1 kHz range.

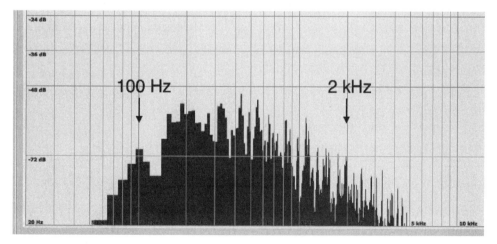

Figure 5-21. The spectrum of the acoustic guitar.

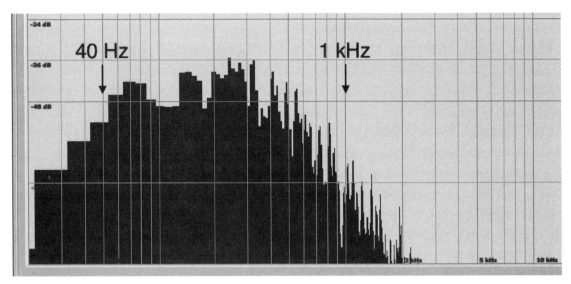

Figure 5-22. The spectrum of the electric piano.

We can use filters to remove some of the frequencies from each instrument to leave space for the other one to come through. First we will pass the acoustic guitar through a *high-pass filter*, which lets the high frequencies pass and *attenuates* (turns down) frequencies below a specific point, called the *cut-off frequency*, which we will set to 400 Hz.

A *low-pass* filter could be used on the electric piano. It will let the frequencies below the cut-off frequency pass while it attenuates the frequencies above. To make things simple, we will set the cut-off frequency for this example to the same 400 Hz. Using these two filters will create a separate area in the spectrum for each instrument to come through. The guitar will be strongest above 400 Hz, and the electric piano will predominate below 400 Hz. Take care not to ruin the sound of instruments by filtering them too much. Video Example 5-5 demonstrates this process.

VIDEO EXAMPLE 5-5. Creating space in the spectrum for the two instruments.

EXERCISE 5-5: *Set up a high-pass filter on the guitar and a low-pass filter on the electric piano in overlap.song.*

Figure 5-23 shows the clarity obtained from carving out a space in the spectrum for each instrument, as compared with the original masking shown in Figure 5-19. The guitar can now be more clearly heard in Audio Example 5-15.

AUDIO EXAMPLE 5-15. The filtered guitar and electric piano. Compare with the unfiltered version in Audio Example 5-13.

AUDIO EXAMPLE 5-13. Unfiltered guitar and electric piano.

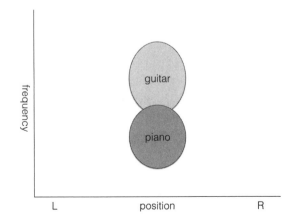

Figure 5-23. A soundstage plot showing the electric piano and guitar separated by differences in tone.

To get the maximum amount of separation, we could combine the two techniques—pan the two instruments apart and add our filters (Figure 5-24), as demonstrated in Video Example 5-6 and heard in Audio Example 5-16.

AUDIO EXAMPLE 5-16. The filtered guitar and electric piano have been panned apart.

VIDEO EXAMPLE 5-6. The guitar and electric piano filtered and panned apart.

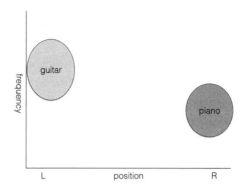

Figure 5-24. A soundstage plot showing the electric piano and guitar separated by differences in tone and location.

EXERCISE 5-6: *Pan the filtered guitar and piano apart in the separated.song file.*

Review the four approaches we've just seen to compare some of the options an engineer has to blend and separate tracks. Which one do you like best from Audio Examples 5-13 to 5-16? Why?

AUDIO EXAMPLE 5-13 (unfiltered/mono).

AUDIO EXAMPLE 5-14 (unfiltered/stereo).

AUDIO EXAMPLE 5-15 (filtered/mono).

AUDIO EXAMPLE 5-16 (filtered/stereo).

Remember: Try to get the right tone with microphone placement and performance technique, and then use EQs to make slight adjustments after the fact if necessary. Aiming a mic at the bridge of the guitar will give you a brighter sound, as will strumming closer to the bridge. Playing away from the bridge and putting the mic over the 12th fret will give you a mellower sound.

Low-pass filters can also be used to reduce high-frequency noise components heard when playing vinyl records and analog tapes or recordings made in noisy spaces. An excerpt from a recording of a speech about loyalty given by Woodrow Wilson's Secretary of State Bainbridge Colby is heard in Audio Example 5-17, one in a series of 59 sound recordings made by Guy Golterman with early Columbia Gramophone equipment between 1918 and 1922 of national and world leaders (courtesy of Ed Golterman). The surface noise of the disc can be reduced by passing it through a low-pass filter.

AUDIO EXAMPLE 5-17. Historic recording.

VIDEO EXAMPLE 5-7. Reducing hiss and pops with a low-pass filter.

EXERCISE 5-7: *Reduce the hiss and pops in the bainbridge.song session file.*

The last type of filter we'll look out here is a *band-pass* filter. The band-pass filter can either boost or cut a band of frequencies situated around a *center frequency*. The Q or *resonance* of the filter defines the narrowness of the band. A high Q value makes the band narrow.

VIDEO EXAMPLE 5-8. Adjusting the parameters of Studio One's Channel Strip midband peaking filter.

EXERCISE 5-8: *Experiment with moving the center frequency of a band-pass filter, using your mix from Exercise 5-7.*

Answer quiz questions 5.6–5.8.

Frequency Bands

Some amplifiers have tone controls to boost or cut treble and bass frequencies. These are designed to give listeners the ability to make simple adjustments to their systems—for example, so that people who do not hear high frequencies well can brighten the sound, or to adjust for room acoustics and speaker placement.

VIDEO EXAMPLE 5-9. The effect of turning up and down the bass and treble control knobs of an amplifier can be simulated by adjusting the levels of two tracks of an audio session with the appropriate filter settings. The low and high shelf filters of Studio One's Channel Strip are used here.

EXERCISE 5-9: *Experiment with bass and treble controls.*

Some loudspeakers have more than one driver. One of the benefits of this design is that each element can concentrate on reproducing frequencies in one range. The signal that comes into the speaker is divided into three frequency bands by a *crossover*. In the three-way Event 2030 speaker shown in Figure 5-25, bass frequencies up to 400 Hz are sent to the large *woofer*, the mid-range frequencies from 400 Hz to 3 kHz to the mid-range driver, and the high frequencies above 3 kHz to the tiny *tweeter*. When the three drivers are playing together, a full-range experience is created for the listener (Video Example 5-10).

Figure 5-25. A crossover system divides the signal into a different range of frequencies for each driver.

VIDEO EXAMPLE 5-10. The contributions of each of the drivers in a three-way system can be simulated in a DAW. The same music is played on each track. Track 1 has a low-pass filter letting frequencies below 400 Hz pass. Track 2 has a band-pass filter letting the frequencies from 400 Hz to 3 kHz pass. Track 3 has a high-pass filter that lets frequencies above 3 kHz pass. The low and high shelf filters and midband peaking filter of Studio One's Channel Strip are used here.

EXERCISE 5-10: *Listen to the three frequency bands in the 3-way.song session one by one and then together. Listen carefully to what each band contributes to the spectrum.*

Answer quiz question 5.9.

It can be very helpful for engineers to develop their sensitivity and awareness of frequency bands, so that they can more quickly and effectively set up and adjust filters to make desired changes in tone. Those who can pick out fine details in music are said to have "golden ears." Make sure you can hear the difference between low and high frequencies and then move on two, three, and more bands.

Remember that the range of frequencies that humans can hear extends from about 20 Hz to about 20 kHz. The room that you're listening in and choice of speakers or headphones make a big difference in the resulting tone. One way to help calibrate your ears is to listen to gold standard recordings that you are familiar with in the same style of music that you're working on. Putting your music side by side with *reference mixes* made by the pros can be intimidating, but it gives you a point of reference.

Here is one set of frequencies that could be used to divide the audible spectrum into four layers:

Lows (20 Hz–120 Hz). These frequencies may be felt more than heard, and give power to kick drum and bass guitar. Too little here makes the music sound thin; too much makes it boomy.

Low-mids (120 Hz–2 kHz). Fundamental frequencies and low-numbered overtones of many instruments and voices are located here, providing the "meat" of the music. The right amount makes the music warm and full. Too much turns it muddy.

High-mids (2 kHz–4 kHz). This range provides much of the definition and presence in music, and the intelligibility of words, since the transients of consonants happen here. Too much can make things sound piercing and harsh.

Highs (4 kHz–20 kHz). These frequencies provide brilliance, sparkle, and air.

VIDEO EXAMPLE 5-11. How to use low, low-mid, high-mid, and high-frequency controls.

EXERCISE 5-11: *Observe what each of the four frequency bands contributes to the spectrum in the 4-way.song session.*

Answer quiz question 5.10.

Working with Instruments

The *solo* function on a mixer makes it possible to listen to one or more tracks by themselves. Whenever the solo button is clicked, the other tracks in the song are silenced until the button is turned off by clicking it again. An alternative method to listening to certain tracks is to click on the *mute* button of any track you don't want to hear. The use of solo and mute buttons is demonstrated in Video Example 5-12.

VIDEO EXAMPLE 5-12. Function of solo and mute buttons.

EXERCISE 5-12: *Try the solo and mute buttons in the 4-way.song session.*

We now turn our attention to controlling the tone of the some of the most frequently used instruments in popular music, beginning with the kick drum. Its large drumhead produces a low fundamental frequency, and the transients caused by the beater striking it produce overtones across the spectrum. The way the kick is EQed depends on the tone the engineer wants for the mix. The thud from the resonating chamber that is popular in hip-hop and dance music can be found below 60–90 Hz. The attack from the beater is located around 700 Hz, and the snap around 2 kHz (Video Example 5-13).

VIDEO EXAMPLE 5-13. Adjusting the tone of a kick drum.

EXERCISE 5-13: *Adjust the tone of the kick drum in the kick.song session.*

Answer quiz question 5.11.

The other primary member of the drum set is the snare drum. The Shure SM57 is a popular mic for recording it and is usually placed a few inches away, pointing toward the inside of the rim, out of the way so that the drummer won't hit it. Depending on how the snare drum is tuned, the core of its sound lies somewhere around 150 Hz. *Resonance* refers to a boosting of a particular range of frequencies created by the shape and size of the space within which a pressure wave is traveling. A band-pass filter can boost or cut a frequency band, making it a useful tool to turn down a resonant frequency.

VIDEO EXAMPLE 5-14. Turning down the resonant frequency of a snare drum.

EXERCISE 5-14: *Find the resonant frequency in the snare.song file.*

In Chapter 1 we saw how the proximity effect occurs when a condenser microphone is placed within inches of a source, as heard in Audio Example 1-12. The solution suggested at that time was to engage the bass roll-off switch on the mic, if it had one.

AUDIO EXAMPLE 1-12. The proximity effect causes a buildup of bass frequencies.

Some engineers prefer to make changes to EQ rather than use the roll-off switch. Plugging in a high-pass filter perform the same sort of compensation for the boost in low frequencies. Video Example 5-15 shows how a high-pass filter can be used for this job.

VIDEO EXAMPLE 5-15. Using a high-pass filter to compensate for the proximity effect.

EXERCISE 5-15: *Use a high-pass filter on the guitar in proximity.song to tame the boominess.*

Boosting and cutting the amplitude of frequency bands is possible only if there is energy there to begin with. High-pass filtering a ukulele track with a low cut-off frequency would have no effect, since there are no frequencies below it to cut out. Video Example 5-16 shows how high to set the high-pass frequency of a high-pitched instrument like the ukulele, should that be necessary.

VIDEO EXAMPLE 5-16. Setting the cut-off point for a ukulele.

EXERCISE 5-16: *High-pass filter the ukulele in ukulele.song.*

Studio One has a number of FX Chains—combinations of effects that can be loaded in as one unit from the browser. It can be interesting to see what the designers have set up and then to adjust the parameters to fit the specific characteristics of your track. Many of Studio One's filters are combined with compressors and other dynamic processors in a single plug-in. This saves space and makes it easier to go back and forth between adjusting tone and volume, which happens often since a change in one affects the choices made for the other. For example, a slow attack on a compressor will let more of the initial high-frequency transients of a snare drum hit pass through before the compressor turns the volume down, making the sound brighter.

VIDEO EXAMPLE 5-17. Using an FX Chain on a vocal track.

EXERCISE 5-17: *Open the sacred-voice.song session file and experiment with the plug-in settings, especially those in the EQ section.*

Listen to the track in context with the other tracks. What sounds good on a track when it is soloed may not work as well in a mix.

REVIEW

Tone is the quality of sound that helps the listener identify which instrument or voice is responsible for a sound. Tone quality influences our perception of intimacy, since the closer a sound source is to us, the brighter it is. We can also detect the emotional state of a singer or speaker by tone of voice.

Most sounds we hear are made from a large number of sine wave components of different frequencies and amplitudes. The graph of a spectrum allows us to see the frequencies and amplitudes of the components and confirm what the effect is of a filter on a signal that passes through it. Filters cut or boost certain frequency ranges and are the main tool engineers have to change tone after it has been recorded. The best way to control tone is to start in the studio, get the right sound quality in the room, and put an appropriate microphone in the right spot. That way, fewer adjustments have to be made later.

We've made a few experiments in changing the tone of instruments in the rhythm section and vocals. Pay close attention to the tone of sounds heard throughout the day in your environment and how it changes depending on your location. Be aware of the tones that have been created on your favorite recordings. Experiment with changing EQ settings on tracks while listening to them in solo mode and also in context with the rest of a band. As you become more aware of tone and how it is produced by changes in the amplitude of individual frequency bands, you will be better able to find the right place for a microphone and make EQ changes to create a tonal balance that is right for the music you want to produce.

ACTIVITIES

The following activities will give you a chance to practice manipulating the spectrum of recordings. Start paying more attention to how the tone changes depending on the placement of microphones while recording and EQ settings during the mixing phase. Notice how there are changes of tone in your environment, and in the music you listen to.

Basic

1. Open the kick-bass.song session. Make three copies of the bass track and mute the original. Put a different plug-in on each of the duplicated tracks: Channel Strip on the first, Fat Channel on the second, and Pro EQ on the third. Solo one at a time and change the tone for each.

2. Review the notes you took on the differences in tone between the three instruments in Audio Example 5-1. Do you hear any new details now that you've become more aware of spectrum? If you're using the Artist or above version of Studio One, open the file in dynamic-spectrum.song, open the Spectrum Meter on the Main Out, and pay attention to how the tone changes over time. Watch Video Example 5-18 if you are using Studio One Free, since it doesn't include the Spectrum Meter. Which instrument's higher-energy components die out over time? Which instrument has the most high-frequency components?

AUDIO EXAMPLE 5-1. A flute, a piano, and an accordion.

VIDEO EXAMPLE 5-18. Observe the changes in the spectrum over time.

Intermediate

1. Set up a recording session, paying special attention to how the musicians sound in the room, where microphones are placed, and how the raw tracks sound when listening on your monitoring system before any equalization is added. Write down your observations and note any differences you hear between the sounds in the room where the musicians are and what you're hearing through the recording system. When you're done recording, set a good balance between the tracks. Listen carefully to each track and what it contributes to the combined mix. Pick one element that you think could be improved with an EQ plug-in. Make that change and take notes about what the situation was, what you tried to change, what you did to change it, how it was changed, and what you might do differently the next time you record something.

2. Open the sacred-drums-percussion.song session. It has the individual tracks of drums and percussion, organized in folders and submixes provided by Tim Leitner, the engineer, by how they could be mixed down to stereo pairs. Solo each of the submixes, listen, then mute them and listen to the individual tracks that were mixed together to create them. See how close you can get to creating a similar sound through volume balancing, panning, and adding EQ.

Advanced

1. Record something new over the drum and/or percussion submixes or individual tracks from the sacred-drums-percussion.song session. Explore the effects you can create with Studio One's EQ plug-ins on selected tracks and the main mix.

2. Experiment with PreSonus's RedlightDist analog distortion emulator.

3. Listen to everything as much as possible.

FOR FURTHER EXPLORATION

+ Bill Gibson, *Microphones & Mixers*, second edition. *Hal Leonard Recording Method*, Book 1. Montclair, NJ: Hal Leonard Corporation, 2011. Chapter 1: "Sound Theory," Chapter 4: "Signal Path," and Chapter 7: "Effects."

+ Roey Izhaki, *Mixing Audio: Concepts, Practices and Tools*. Waltham, MA: Focal Press, 2012. Chapter 14 on equalizers.

Develop your ability to identify specific frequency bands:

+ Morton Laboratories' "Golden Ears" ear-training course

+ Harman International's (free) "How to Listen" software

QUIZ QUESTIONS

5.1: Which tone goes with which spectrum?

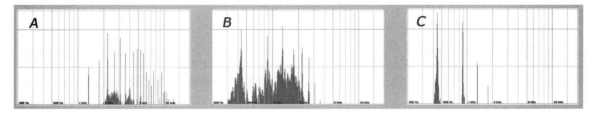

Figure 5-26. Three spectra.

AUDIO EXAMPLE 5-18. Tone 1.

AUDIO EXAMPLE 5-19. Tone 2.

AUDIO EXAMPLE 5-20. Tone 3.

5.2: What does the graph of a spectrum show you? What is graphed on the horizontal and vertical axes?

5.3: What does the graph of a waveform show you? What is graphed on the horizontal and vertical axes?

5.4: What aspect of mixing could be helped by looking at the graph of the music's spectrum?

5.5: When editing, why does looking at the graph of the music's waveform help you more than a graph of its spectrum?

5.6: What's the name of the type of filter that cuts out frequencies above the cut-off frequency?

5.7: What's the name of the type of filter that cuts out frequencies below the cut-off frequency?

5.8: What's the name of the type of filter that boost or cuts frequencies around a center frequency?

5.9: Listen to the Audio Example 5-21 and then and match Audio Examples 5-22 to 5-24 with the frequency band of the band-pass filter through which the original was boosted:

AUDIO EXAMPLE 5-21. The original, unfiltered recording.

AUDIO EXAMPLE 5-22.

AUDIO EXAMPLE 5-23.

AUDIO EXAMPLE 5-24.

Frequency band 1: 20 Hz–400 Hz.
Frequency band 2: 400 Hz–3 kHz.
Frequency band 3: 3 kHz–20 kHz.

5.10: Listen to the Audio Example 5-25 and then and match Audio Examples 5-26 to 5-29 with the frequency band of the band-pass filter through which the original has been boosted:

AUDIO EXAMPLE 5-25. The original, unfiltered recording.

AUDIO EXAMPLE 5-26.

AUDIO EXAMPLE 5-27.

AUDIO EXAMPLE 5-28.

AUDIO EXAMPLE 5-29.

Frequency band 1: 20 Hz–120 Hz.
Frequency band 2: 120 Hz–2 kHz.
Frequency band 3: 2 kHz–4 kHz.
Frequency band 4: 4 kHz–20 kHz.

5.11: Which of these two recordings of a kick drum has greater energy in the 700 Hz range?

AUDIO EXAMPLE 5-30.

AUDIO EXAMPLE 5-31.

Answers to the quiz questions can be found in Appendix C.

STUDIO ONE SHORTCUTS

Ctrl/Cmd + click on a knob to return it to the 0 position.

AMBIENCE

GOAL AND OBJECTIVES

After working through this chapter, you should be able to create an impression of different listening environments and control the location of parts located within it.

+ Change the settings of reverberation processors to change the size of the perceived space.

+ Balance between wet and dry signals to create a feeling of distance.

+ Understand the signal flow of inserted plug-ins.

+ Explain the difference between echo and reverberation.

PREREQUISITES

+ Understand terms such as waveform, amplitude, gain, dB, and compression.

+ Know how to insert effects and understand what compression does (Chapter 2).

+ Understand how to automate volume after working with "Easy Street" (Chapter 3).

+ Understand what bus channels are and how to work with them in the Console view (Chapter 3).

+ Understand what a filter is and how it affects tone (Chapter 5).

THEORY AND PRACTICE

In Chapter 5, we looked at some frequency-based effects that can be used to modify tone. In this chapter, we will look at time-based effects, such as reverberation and echo, that use delays to create a sense of space and dimension in music productions. In the old days, audio engineers used vibrating objects like springs and plates to prolong vibrations. Today the delayed signals are calculated with computer algorithms in software plug-ins.

Imagine a pressure wave expanding like a balloon in a space. We call the part that reaches the listener's ears in a straight line from the vibrating object without bouncing off any surfaces the *direct sound*. When the pressure wave reaches a wall, floor, or ceiling, it reflects off the surface and reaches the listener's ears a little later than the direct sound due to the additional distance it has traveled. This is called the *reflected sound*. The extra time it takes for the sound to reach the listener depends on the length of the path that the wave travels. The air the wave travels through acts like a filter, since the amount of energy that is absorbed depends on the frequency. The surfaces it bounces off of change the tone as well, since different materials reflect certain frequencies better than others.

Ambience

This section is about *ambience*, a word that has two overlapping definitions:

1. The atmosphere of a place that results from its sights, smells, and sounds.

2. Background noise or reverberation that is added to a recording to create an impression that it was recorded live in a particular place.

As we have said before, volume is the parameter in music that the general public has the most practical experience with. Like tone, ambience is something that listeners are sensitive to but not very consciously aware of. Doing a few quick exercises may help you focus on how ambience can be used to add to the listener's enjoyment of music.

Close one eye and look around you for a minute. Try reaching out and touching an object with your finger. Notice how much easier this is to do when you open your other eye and have the stereoscopic depth perception made possible by looking at the same object from two slightly different angles.

Next, notice the behavior of sounds in your room. Close one ear and listen for a minute while paying attention to where the sounds are coming from. Now open both ears and listen some more. Notice how the stereophonic perception that results from listening to the same sound source with two ears in slightly different positions gives you more information about the locations of sound sources. Listening with two ears gives you a stereophonic experience, like the sense of depth you get from looking at objects with two eyes.

Move close to a wall and touch it. Close your eyes. Move your head close to and away from the wall. Staying in contact with the wall with your hand should reduce the likelihood of hitting it with your head. Find a partner to help you if you have any doubt that you can do this safely. Can you tell when you are getting close to the wall, through subtle changes in ambience? Some people have developed the ability to navigate through an environment using echolocation, by listening to the reflections off nearby objects of clicks and tapping sounds.

Now close your eyes and have a partner lead you into a series of different acoustic environments. Listen to the changes in ambience as you move from one space to another.

Musical styles have evolved along with the spaces in which music is played. Gregorian chant developed in the Middle Ages in reverberant spaces where the notes the monks sang hung in the air and slowly died out (Audio Example 6-1).

AUDIO EXAMPLE 6-1. Gregorian chant.

Imagine this type of music sung on a beach or in a car, or played on headphones. The space would not supply any of the natural sustain of the cathedral. Today the creation of ambient effects is usually given over to the recording engineer.

Reverberation

Reverberation (or *reverb* for short) is caused by a mass of delayed reflections arriving from the multiple surfaces in a room, so many and so dense that we do not pick them out individually. The reverberation of the cathedral is what causes the notes of the Gregorian chant to be sustained. When a vibration pattern begins in a room, a pressure wave spreads out and the direct sound from it is the first to reach the listener. Soon the indirect sound starts to arrive. It is the part of the pressure wave that has reflected off the walls, floor, ceiling, and any objects in the room. The *decay time* of reverberation is defined as the time it takes for the amplitude of the reverb to drop by 60 dB.

Compare the amount of reverberation and tone changes in the following recordings of a piano from different distances as heard in Chapter 1. It is not until you are a ways back that you become aware that the performances took place in a large auditorium.

AUDIO EXAMPLE 6-2. One foot away from piano.

AUDIO EXAMPLE 6-3. Four feet away onstage.

AUDIO EXAMPLE 6-4. 10 feet away onstage.

AUDIO EXAMPLE 6-5. First row.

AUDIO EXAMPLE 6-6. Third row.

AUDIO EXAMPLE 6-7. Middle row.

AUDIO EXAMPLE 6-8. Back row.

We often choose to record popular music in studios with smaller rooms than the spaces used to perform for an audience. Recording with microphones close to the instruments provides the strongest signal and most detailed sound. Since the direct sound in the microphones is so much louder than the reflected sound, the acoustics of the room are effectively eliminated. This is why the acoustics of the auditorium have no effect on the recording of the grand piano when the microphone is only one foot away (Audio Example 6-2).

One reason to add reverb to a song is to make it sound like it was recorded in a particular sonic environment. One way to create natural reverberation is to set up an extra microphone farther back in the room, away from the instruments, and to record this *room mic*. Instead of using artificial reverberation, the ambience is created by blending the room mic with the dry close-miked tracks, and the effect creates a sense of space.

VIDEO EXAMPLE 6-1. A single room mic can be blended with close-miked drums.

EXERCISE 6-1: *Balance the room mic in the room-mic-drums.song session.*

The most important controls for the reverb plug-in are the room size, which determines how long the reverb will last; and *wet/dry balance*, which controls how much of the processed (wet) signal will come through relative to the amount of unprocessed (dry) signal. For example, if the wet/dry balance of a reverb plug-in is set to 20 percent, it means that 20 percent of what comes out of the reverb unit has been reverberated and the rest is unreverberated (dry). The signal flow diagram shows the function of the wet/dry knob, which sets the balance between the amount of the input that is sent through the reverb process and the part that is passed through unchanged.

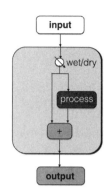

Figure 6-1. The function of the wet/dry knob in a reverb processor.

Studio One Artist has two reverb plug-ins that provide a wide range of effects: MixVerb and Room Reverb. MixVerb (Figure 6-2) is a simple plug-in to use because of its limited number of controls: predelay, size, dampening, and a gate. The last section has a stereo width control and mix knob to control the wet/dry balance. It is the best choice for a plug-in if you're going to insert reverb on a number of individual tracks because of its computational efficiency.

Figure 6-2. The MixVerb plug-in.

The closer the control is to the dry side, the more input sound that will be passed through without processing (Audio Examples 6-9 and 6-10). The further the control is set to the wet side, the more the effect sound will be heard (Audio Examples 6-11 and 6-12).

AUDIO EXAMPLE 6-9. A wet/dry mix of zero percent has no effect applied.

AUDIO EXAMPLE 6-10. A wet/dry mix of around 20 percent creates a subtle effect.

AUDIO EXAMPLE 6-11. A wet/dry mix of 50 percent is heavy on effect. The greater the size of the room, the more obvious it will be.

AUDIO EXAMPLE 6-12. A wet/dry mix of 100 percent means that the output is completely wet, with none of the dry input mixed in.

VIDEO EXAMPLE 6-2. Adjusting the wet/dry balance.

EXERCISE 6-2: *Adjust the wet/dry balance in the mixverb-drums.song session file.*

Room Reverb is the more advanced reverb plug-in in the Artist version of Studio One. Since it uses more CPU resources, it is more efficient to set up a single dedicated FX Channel for it and then send multiple signals from other tracks to it, rather than inserting a copy of the plug-in on all the individual tracks. The Room Reverb plug-in window helps visualize changes in the room's dimensions as you adjust its size, width, and height (Figure 6-3). Distance refers to the separation of the listener from the sound source. There are some unusual options included in the Character section: Dampness (humidity), Population (number of listeners in the audience soaking up bass frequencies), and Reflectivity (smoothness of surfaces). The Length setting controls the length of time the reverb hangs on after the input sound stops. The Mix knob in Room Reverb adjusts the mix of reverb tail and early reflections, while the Send knob sets the wet/dry mix of the overall reverb with the original input.

Figure 6-3. The Room Reverb plug-in window.

Answer quiz questions 6.1–6.4, found at the end of the chapter.

Sounds on tracks with a low wet/dry ratio will seem to be closer to the listener than those with a higher ratio. This is due to experience we have built up about the world, like the recordings from the microphone at increasing distances from a piano in an auditorium heard in Audio Examples 6-2 to 6-8. The impression of distance can also be helped with EQ. The closer objects are, the more high frequencies they have, since high frequencies are absorbed more as pressure waves pass through air.

VIDEO EXAMPLE 6-3. Adding reverb to some tracks and not others creates depth.

EXERCISE 6-3: *Listen to the effect of taking the reverb off the guitar in mixverb-bus.song.*

AUDIO EXAMPLE 6-13. The guitar has the same reverb as the rest of the group.

AUDIO EXAMPLE 6-14. The guitar is the only instrument not to have reverb. Does that make it sound closer to you?

Does it seem to you like the reverb-free guitar in the second example is closer to you than when it has reverb like the rest of the instruments? Remember that high frequencies are absorbed more than lows as the pressure wave travels through the air. Raising the amplitude of the guitar's high frequencies a little makes it seem even closer (Video Example 6-4).

VIDEO EXAMPLE 6-4. Adding some high frequencies to bring the guitar forward in the mix.

EXERCISE 6-4: *Brighten the guitar's EQ and add reverb to everything else in the mixverb-bus.song session to move the guitar forward.*

Answer quiz question 6.5.

Localization

We have seen how adding reverb can simulate different-size rooms and that varying the balance between the direct and indirect sound of an instrument can move it forward or back in the mix. Next we will learn to be more precise with *localization* effects, which are a result of the listeners' preconscious activity as they judge the distance and direction of a sound source. Being able to determine where sounds are in the environment is an important skill for survival, dating back to when hunters searched for prey. Today we use it to avoid being hit by passing cars, and to create three-dimensional audio mixes. You can test your localization abilities by closing your eyes and moving your hand all around you while you are snapping or rubbing your fingers together. How does the sound change?

The brain uses several cues to localize sounds. Sounds that are coming from directly in front of you arrive at both ears at the same time, with the same amplitude and tone. As the source moves to your left, the sound arrives at your left ear sooner, louder, and brighter than it does at your right ear. Your brain compares the two signals to figure out where the sound is coming from. It's harder to localize sound with one ear, just as it's harder to perceive depth with only one eye. Left and right perception is easier than front and back. Sometimes we turn our heads to give the brain more information. Turning your head while wearing headphones doesn't have any effect on the sound, so your brain arrives at the only possible conclusion: that the sound must be coming from inside your head.

Short Delays

One way to move sounds in the stereo field is with the pan control on the mixer, which changes the proportion in volume levels between two speakers. Sounds heard more loudly from one speaker seem to originate from that side while those that are heard equally loudly from both speakers appear to be in the middle. This works because, in nature, sounds that are on our left side are closer to the left ear. As they pass around the head, they travel an extra distance and lose some amplitude—especially those of higher frequencies that do not bend around objects as well as the lower frequencies do. In addition, sounds that travel around the head arrive at the ear on the other side later.

Presenting a sound in one speaker and then delaying it 1 to 40 milliseconds (ms) later in the other speaker creates a psychoacoustic effect called the *precedence* or *Haas effect*. The listener's brain decides it will interpret this situation as being caused by a single sound source on the undelayed side of the sound field. The more delay there is, the greater the spacious sensation that will be created (Audio Example 6-15, Video Example 6-5), until at some point the effect breaks down and an echo is heard (Audio Example 6-16).

AUDIO EXAMPLE 6-15. Beginning with a guitar in the right speaker with no delay, and then at 0:11 adding a copy of the guitar in the left speaker delayed by 20 ms, which creates a pseudo stereo effect.

AUDIO EXAMPLE 6-16. The delay in the left speaker has been increased to 80 ms, and the effect starts to break down.

VIDEO EXAMPLE 6-5. Creating the Haas effect.

EXERCISE 6-5: *Vary the amount of delay time on the left track in the haas.song session.*

Chorus

Delay can also be used to increase the richness of a sound—a technique that has been used by musicians for thousands of years when they perform in groups. When instruments or voices play roughly the same tone and pitch together, their combined sound is perceived as a section, like a string ensemble or chorus of singers. As the number of available tracks on tape recorders grew over time, engineers increasingly *double-tracked* vocals, instrumental hooks, rhythm guitar parts, and solos. This can be done by having a player listen to his or her performance and record another take as close as possible to the first, so as to not be obvious to the listener what is going on. Mixing the two tracks results in a fatter sound, because of the rub caused by the inevitable slight variations of pitch, tone, and timing between the two versions.

Artificial double-tracking was reportedly discovered in 1966 during the recording of the Beatles' *Revolver* album. John Lennon had become tired of doubling his vocal parts, and Ken Townsend came up with the idea of duplicating Lennon's singing with a second tape recorder whose speed was manipulated to go in and out of sync with the first. The use of doubling to create richness is demonstrated in Chapter 3 with the song "Easy Street," on which Ken Scott assigned most of the tracks to the center, and only panned apart double-tracked parts.

Ensemble-type effects can also be created electronically by passing signals through a *chorus* plug-in that mixes the input sound with one or more delayed copies whose pitches are slightly detuned with a slight vibrato.

The Chorus plug-in (Figure 6-4) in Studio One offers four basic controls: Delay (2–20 ms), Speed (the rate of vibrato, 0.01–10 Hz), Width (how much out of tune the delays get), and Depth (the stereo spread).

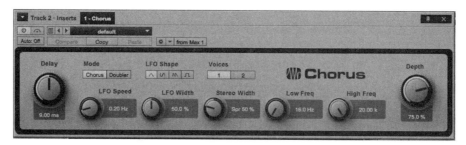

Figure 6-4. The Chorus plug-in.

Compare the sound of an electric piano with and without a chorus effect in Video Example 6-6.

VIDEO EXAMPLE 6-6. Electric piano with and without a chorus effect.

EXERCISE 6-6: *Try out the controls of the Chorus plug-in using the chorus.song session file.*

Echo

An *echo* is created when the direct and delayed versions of a sound are more than 40 ms apart, long enough that they are perceived as separate audio events. Studio One Artist has two delay plug-ins that can be used to create echoes: Analog Delay (Figure 6-5) and Beat Delay (Figure 6-6).

Figure 6-5. The Analog Delay plug-in. Turning off the sync function allows you to set delay times by a number of ms.

Figure 6-6. The Beat Delay plug-in.

The Beat Delay plug-in takes its name from its ability to synchronize the length of a delay with the duration of a note at the current tempo, as demonstrated in Video Example 6-7.

VIDEO EXAMPLE 6-7. Beat Delay synchronized to the metronome.

EXERCISE 6-7: *Try out different note values for delay times in the beat-delay.song session.*

A delay of approximately 75 to 250 ms creates a *slapback* echo, an effect that was associated with 1950s rock-and-roll records from Sam Phillips at Sun Records.

VIDEO EXAMPLE 6-8. How to use the Beat Delay plug-in to create a slapback echo.

EXERCISE 6-8: *Create a slapback echo for the slapback.song session.*

Global Effects

So far we have seen effects plugged into individual tracks. We can also create *global effects* by inserting them into the Main Out, the last point in the mixer where the sound passes before being sent out to headphones and loudspeakers. Effects inserted on the Main Out affect all the tracks of a mix equally. We also have the option to have more than one effect on the same track—for example, inserting an EQ followed by a compressor. When there is more than one effect on the same track, the processes are performed in order from top to bottom, as demonstrated in Video Example 6-9.

VIDEO EXAMPLE 6-9. How to plug in an EQ, reverb, and limiter on the Main output bus.

EXERCISE 6-9: *Add global effects to the main-out.song session file.*

Answer quiz questions 6.6 and 6.7.

Binaural Recording

One problem with creating spatial effects is that there is such a great variety of listeners' playback conditions, such as the size and shape of their rooms and their positions relative to the loudspeakers. *Binaural* recordings designed for listening with headphones are intended to address that problem by reducing the number of variables and offer an engineer the most controlled conditions for creating realistic experiences. Binaural recordings can be made with a dummy head—a simplified model of a human head with microphones mounted where a person's ears would be. When the listener plays the recording back with headphones, the differences in timing, amplitude, and tone fed to each ear can create vivid impressions of the ambience of the original recording site and the location of the listener relative to the sound sources.

Mark Summerell (a.k.a. Clearwing) makes his binaural recordings with a Soundman OKM II headset microphone—a pair of tiny omnidirectional electret condenser mics embedded in molded-plastic earbuds that are worn in his own ears. The outputs of the two microphones are passed through a Soundman A3 adapter and then recorded on a portable Zoom H4n. Mark explains why he incorporates environmental recordings into his ambient music compositions:

> Ambient music has little or no rhythm, so you can't dance, nod your head, or tap your fingers to it. You're forced to focus on nothing but the notes, their pace (or lack thereof), and the simple honesty. It combines well with field recordings of the world exactly as it is, which add a sense of place and are never out of key. I use a lot of customized plug-in chains with delays, reverse delays, and extra-long reverbs to process the ambient music to make its atmosphere, emotion, and spatial placement fit with the environmental sounds. I had an EDM-style track that reminded me of the aftereffects of being in a club, with my ears ringing and every sound muffled, and decided to pair it with a recording I'd made of birds [Audio Example 6-17] in order to re-create the experience of walking home in the early hours of the morning after a long night out.

AUDIO EXAMPLE 6-17. Listen to Summerell's binaural recording of English birdsong with headphones or earbuds.

AUDIO EXAMPLE 6-18. This ambient music composition "Sunken Lane" is designed for binaural playback.

Describe the differences of tone and ambience that you hear in the environmental (Audio Example 6-17) and instrumental tracks (Audio Example 6-18). How well do you think the two worlds combine?

Answer quiz questions 6.8–6.11.

REVIEW

A number of factors change the way music sounds when played back through loudspeakers, including the quality of the speakers and their arrangement in the room, where the listener is positioned relative to them, and the acoustics of the room. This prevents the engineer from being able to create precise spatial effects, because every listening situation is different. Binaural recordings provide the most reliable results because the variations of the room response and the listener's position are eliminated.

The ambience of a recording defines an acoustical space. Listeners determine how far away an object is by the ratio of its reflected (wet) sound to the direct (dry) sound. The prolongation of sounds in a space is called reverberation, and is caused by a mass of countless delayed sounds arriving from different directions. The bigger the room, the longer it takes for the reverberation to die out.

An echo is experienced as a separate acoustic event when sounds arrive at a listener's ears more than about 40 ms apart. Shorter delays can influence the way a listener localizes a sound source, known as the Haas effect. Time- and frequency-modulated delays can also be used to create chorus, phaser, and flanger effects.

Understanding signal flow is fundamental to any audio production situation, from the way pieces of equipment are wired together to the virtual paths that data travels within recording software. In this chapter, we looked at how the wet/dry mix knob works and compared inserting plug-ins on individual channels with global effects on the Main Out channel.

ACTIVITIES

The following activities will give you a chance to practice paying attention to the natural ambience of the acoustic environments you move through during the day, and the effects that can be created by controlling the parameters of reverb processes while mixing.

Basic

1. Take a notebook and explore a variety of acoustic environments. What sounds do you hear in each, and how does the space affect them? Move around within the space and notice differences that depend on whether you stand in the middle, in a corner, close to a wall, etc. Write down your observations and questions.

2. Insert a MixVerb plug-in on the guitar track of "Evening in Copacabana" in the guitar-copacabana.song session. Decide what room size and wet/dry proportion are appropriate.

3. Plug in an Analog Delay effect on the electric piano track in the chorus.song session file. Which settings of delay time sound the best to you, considering the figures that were played? What setting of wet/dry ratio did you like best? Why?

4. Try different delay and reverb plug-ins on Adam Ezra's voice in "Sacred Ground" in the sacred-voice.song session file. Take notes on the settings and effects you produced that you think fit the song the best. Which others didn't work as well, and why? Compare your recording with the stereo mix created by Tim Leitner.

5. Search for a song that uses a lot of echo or reverb on the lead vocal. What style of music would you say it belongs to? Is the effect typical for that style?

Intermediate

1. Apply global reverb to all the tracks in the guitar-copacabana.song session. What room size seems appropriate to you? Why?

2. Record yourself or someone else playing an instrument, talking, or singing. Plug in a reverb on that track and find a setting for room size and wet/dry balance that creates a pleasing balance. What settings did you like best and why?

3. Record an instrument or voice with the microphone from a few inches away on one track, and the same instrument or voice with the microphone moved back a few feet or more on another track. Compare the two tracks. Do you get a feeling for the type of room the sound was recorded in when the microphone was close up? How about when it was farther away? Try inserting a Beat Delay on the track that was recorded with the microphone up close and see if you can find the settings that make it sound similar to the other track.

4. Record two tracks of the same performance, with one microphone up close and another set up as a room mic five or more feet away. Check that both tracks are panned to the center and then find a balance between the two tracks so that you

hear the performance clearly with the close-up mic and some ambience provided by the room mic. Duplicate the two tracks and try a different arrangement, with one panned all or partway to the left and the other all or partway to the right. Solo one pair of tracks and then the other, and describe the differences between the effects they created.

Advanced

1. Explore the controls included in the Room Reverb plug-in.

2. Record a song with a click track suitable for incorporating Beat Delay. Add Beat Delay to one or more tracks. Create a send and FX Channel for one of your tracks and automate the send level to it, so that you can control when and how much of your track is being delayed. Experiment with different beat lengths for delay time. Automate the playback level of your FX Channel so that you can fade it in and out over time.

3. Experiment with the Chorus, Phaser, and Flanger plug-ins. Which do you like the best and on which type of instruments?

4. Compare the flanging and chorusing effects achievable with the Analog Delay plug-in to those obtained with the dedicated Chorus, Phaser, and Flanger plug-ins. How do the Inertia, Damping, and Width controls affect the sound?

5. Listen to binaural recordings with headphones. Make some of your own to capture the ambience of a variety of different spaces. Take notes about the places you went and what you heard. Play the recordings back for friends and see if they can judge the size and any other qualities of the space in which they were made.

6. Make a script for a short scene of a radio play with two or more characters. Record each voice with binaural microphone system or a single microphone processed with the Binaural Pan plug-in to position the different voices in a variety of locations. Consider adding opening and closing music and sound effects. Listen back wearing headphones. Write down your observations concerning how vivid the natural and plug-in effects were.

FOR FURTHER EXPLORATION

Read the chapter on Built-in Effects in the *Studio One Reference Manual*.
  Online:

* RØDE Microphones' Soundbooth application, found online or downloadable as an iPad app. Experiment with blending the drum room mic with the rest of the set.

QUIZ QUESTIONS

6.1: Which Studio One reverb plug-in is the simplest to use and requires the least amount of system resources?

6.2: How does increasing the Size in a reverb plug-in affect the sound?

6.3: What does the Mix knob do on a reverb plug-in? How do you decide what a good setting for it would be?

6.4: How is the wet/dry mix controlled when using a room mic to add ambience rather than a reverb plug-in?

6.5: How can reverb be used to make instruments on selected tracks sound more distant than the rest of the group?

6.6: Explain a situation in which you decide to insert a global effect on the Main Out.

6.7: Describe a different situation in which an effect would be better applied to an individual channel instead of to the Main Out.

6.8: Why does a recording made with a binaural system sound more realistic played back on headphones than over loudspeakers?

6.9: What is the difference between echo and reverberation?

6.10: Define ambience, direct sound, and reflected sound.

6.11: Brain Buster: Why do you think reverb and echo plug-ins have web/dry controls and EQ filter plug-ins don't?

Answers to the quiz questions can be found in Appendix C.

MIX SESSION: POP AND ROCK

CHAPTER 7

POP AND ROCK STYLES

In this Mix Session chapter, you will have the opportunity to work with one or more songs in the pop and rock styles. You may wish to listen to the stereo mixes to help decide which of the multitracks you want to download first and then jump to the corresponding section for more information on the song and suggestions of things you might try.

There are a lot of tracks in some of these sessions, so you may want to increase the block to make it easier for your computer to keep up (Studio One > Preferences > Audio). The tracks have been colorized and organized in folders for you. If you want to reduce the number of channels in the Console, you can create bus channels, as was done in Chapter 3 with "Easy Street," and then click on the Banks button and hide the tracks you don't need to see while you work on the different sections of the arrangement.

AUDIO EXAMPLE 7-1. Sam Broussard: "Times Like These."

AUDIO EXAMPLE 7-2. Caleb Elliott: "Where You Wanna Be."

AUDIO EXAMPLE 7-3. Adam Ezra: "Sacred Ground."

AUDIO EXAMPLE 7-4. Magda: "Stuck In Between."

AUDIO EXAMPLE 7-5. Robert Willey: "Motherless Child."

AUDIO EXAMPLE 7-6. Ryan Ordway: "Easy Street."

SAM BROUSSARD: "TIMES LIKE THESE"

Sam Broussard is a guitarist living in South Louisiana, the home of Cajun and zydeco music. When he is not out on the road with Steve Riley and the Mamou Playboys, he may be found as a solo act performing his own compositions. An interview with him about the production of "Times Like These" is available on the book's companion website at lovelythinking.com.

STUDIO ONE SESSION FILE: TimesLikeThese.song

Credits

Website: sambroussard.com
Album title: *Veins* (2010)
Recorded by Sam at home except for the drums, which were recorded by Misha Kachkachishvili at Axis Studio (now Esplanade Studios) in New Orleans.
Mixed and mastered by Tony Daigle at Electric Comoland (Lafayette, Louisiana).
Musicians: Sam Broussard, vocals, guitars, fretless bass, fiddle, keyboards; Doug Belote, drums

Suggestions

As with all these songs, your first challenge may be to find a good balance between the drums, bass, guitar, and lead vocals. "Times Like These" adds additional layers of live fiddle parts with sampled strings that need to work together in the same acoustic world. See if you can support Sam's goal when he is arranging "to make all the parts stand up individually and not recede into an unheard support role."

Editing challenge: Create a shorter version appropriate for AM radio play without cutting out any of the words.

CALEB ELLIOTT: "WHERE YOU WANNA BE"

I must have passed Caleb several times in the hall without knowing it when I was a teacher at the University of Louisiana at Lafayette and he was playing cello in the school symphony. He now composes and performs his own original music. An interview with him about "Where You Wanna Be" is on the book's companion website.

STUDIO ONE SESSION FILE: WhereYouWannaBe.song

Credits

Website: calebelliott.com
Album title: *Where You Wanna Be* (2012)
Engineer: Tony Daigle, assisted by Aaron Thomas
Studio: Electric Comoland (Lafayette, Louisiana)
Composer: Caleb Elliott
Executive Producer: Todd Mouton
Musicians: Caleb Elliott, cello, guitar, vocals; Mitch Reed, fiddle; Joe Butts, bass

Suggestions

Create a good blend in the cellos and background singer sections. Experiment with cutting some of the highs off the background vocals and adding the Chorus effect to make them sit back a little in the mix. Spread the cello and string parts out. The punchy background vocals in the verses can be mixed higher than the sustained lines during the prechorus.

Check out the click tracks that Tony Daigle made. Caleb found them much more inspiring to play with than a metronome. Try automating the panning of the background voice answering the title line, as Tony did in his stereo mix.

ADAM EZRA: "SACRED GROUND"

The Adam Ezra Group is a roots-rock band that began in Boston and has since toured with the likes of the Goo Goo Dolls, the Marshall Tucker Band, and Los Lobos. "Sacred Ground" was released on an acoustic album with other songs that don't fit into their live shows. An interview with their engineer, Tim Leitner, can be found on the book's companion website.

STUDIO ONE SESSION FILE: SacredGround.song

Credits

Website: adamezra.com
Album title: *Daniel the Brave* (2012)
Engineer: Tim Leitner
Studio: Howard Schwartz Recording (New York City) and Tim's house
Composer: Adam Ezra
Musicians: Adam Ezra, vocals, acoustic guitar; Turtle, percussion; Alex Martin, drums; Nelson Leong, bass; Josh Gold, keyboard

Suggestions

Automate the levels of the hand percussion to make room for the drums and slide guitar that enter later in the song. Listen to the part the electric guitar is playing and find the proper weight for it in the mix considering its function. See if you can match the tone and presence that the engineer got with the acoustic guitar and vocal. Automate an increase in reverb while fading out the music at the end to move it off into the distance.

MAGDA: "STUCK IN BETWEEN"

Magda is from Kraków, the cultural capital of Poland, where she studied singing at the School of Music.

STUDIO ONE SESSION FILE: StuckInBetween.song

Credits

Engineer: Neil Citron
Composer: Magda
Lyrics: Magda, Matthew Ollar, and Neil Citron
Musicians: Magda, vocals; Neil Citron, guitar, drum machine

Suggestions

Notice the markers for song sections. Try automating the level of the guitars to leave enough space for the singer to come through clearly, especially during the verses on which she is in her lower register. The toms and drums submixes are labeled with Xs. Experiment with panning of individual drum tracks. Compress the toms, bass, and vocals. Add reverb to the kick, snare, toms submix, lead vocal, and guitar submix. Notice how the guitars have a wide image due to them being in stereo and panned apart. Add EQ to the guitars and lead vocal if you wish. Bypass the Dual Pan plug-in on the drum loop and Hammond organ. Can you notice the subtle change in ambience it is creating? The synth part is very soft, but an interesting concept—its whole job is to add some grit and distortion. Neil used some third party plug-ins, such as KVR's UAD 4K Channel Strip and Softube's FET Compress, and some outboard hardware like a Lexicon PCM 60 reverb. References to those can be seen in his original session file StuckInBetweenNeil.song found in the StuckInBetween folder.

ROBERT WILLEY: "MOTHERLESS CHILD"

Information on the author of this book, Robert Willey, is included at the end of this book.

STUDIO ONE SESSION FILE: MotherlessChild.song

Credits

Traditional, arranged and performed by Robert Willey.

Suggestions

The last line of each verse is the refrain: *A long way from home*. It's too low for me to sing, but I just loved the key of B♭m for the song. See what you can do to bring the voice out. Create stereo images out of the mono guitar tracks with the Haas effect.

RYAN ORDWAY: "EASY STREET"

See Chapter 3 for guidance on mixing this song, which was recorded by Ken Scott with the students at the Blackbird Academy.

MIX SESSION: FUNK/SOUL

PHAT HAT: "DA GUV'NAH"

In this Mix Session chapter, you will work with Phat Hat's funk/soul song "Da Guv'nah," which comes as a built-in demo in Studio One. Phat Hat and PreSonus (publishers of Studio One) are headquartered in Baton Rouge, and the song recounts the names of Louisiana's recent governors. Jimmie Davis was a popular country and gospel singer and songwriter and Grammy Award winner who held the office for two nonconsecutive terms. "Da Guv'nah" quotes from "You Are My Sunshine," one of his best-known compositions. It is played here with a traditional New Orleans parade-style second-line groove, the type you may hear played by a brass band in the French Quarter.

The song is distributed as one of the demos inside Studio One. After launching the program and clicking on Demos and Tutorials on the right side of the Start window, you can select "Da Guv'nah."

AUDIO EXAMPLE 8-1. Phat Hat: "Da Guv'nah."

Credits

Engineer: Rick Naqvi
Studio: Black Dog Recording Studio (Baton Rouge, Louisiana)
Composer: Phat Hat
Musicians: Rick Naqvi, guitar; Wendell Woods, lead vocal; Jerry Henderson, bass; John Jones, keyboard; Brad Zell, rhythm guitar, percussion; Andy Pizzo, trombone; Jeff Chatelain, trumpet; Don Thomas, drums

Suggestions

Open up the tracks and check out the plug-ins and their settings, including the global EQ and compression on the Main Out. See what effect the short delay has on the lead vocal. Bypass the effects like the Pro EQ on the top snare drum. Why do you think the effect was used? Notice how the long delay is turned up for the last line. Try automating more spots to add echo like that. Can you find the loop used in the first chorus and pick it out in the mix? During the "You Are My Sunshine" section, try changing the EQ to make it sound like it was recorded in another era. Remix the song without the horns and compare it with the original.

Solo the tracks and listen to the individual tones. Most were recorded through the Studio Live 24.4.2 preamps with little or no EQ or compression. The only exceptions were on the bass guitar, which was recorded through a PreSonus ADL600 preamp and an Empirical Labs Distressor for compression, and the lead vocal, which was recorded through the ADL600 and a Urei 1176LN limiting amplifier for compression.

MIX SESSION: BOSSA NOVA

CHAPTER 9

ALFREDO CARDIM: "EVENING IN COPACABANA"

In this Mix Session chapter, you will have the opportunity to mix a song in the Brazilian bossa nova style. Alfredo Cardim is a Brazilian pianist who lives in Rio de Janeiro, and in this song he describes the atmosphere at one of the city's most famous beaches.

AUDIO EXAMPLE 9-1. Alfredo Cardim: "Evening in Copacabana."

Credits

Website: brazilianpiano.com
Album title: *Brazilian Piano* method (Milwaukee: Hal Leonard Corporation, 2010)
Engineer: Alberto Netto
Studio: Airdrums (Boston, Massachusetts)
Composer: Alfredo Cardim
Musicians: Alfredo Cardim, piano; Barry Smith, bass; Bill Ward, guitar; Renato Malavazi, drums

Suggestions

Trim off the silence at the beginning and the comment at the end. Find a balance that pleases you for the piano, bass, guitar, and percussion. Experiment with different panned positions for the various instruments, including one arrangement with one track of the piano all the way to the left, the other in the middle, the guitar mostly to the right, and the bass and drums in the center. Try another version creating a pseudo stereo effect for the guitar track using the Haas effect, as explained in Chapter 6. Try a Binaural Pan plug-in on the stereo piano and pan it a little to the left. Add a reverb to the Main Out with the right room size and wet/dry mix to add a little extra twinkle to the city lights.

MIX SESSION: ELECTRONICS

10

SONGS

In this Mix Session chapter, you will have the opportunity to mix one or more songs in a variety of electronic styles—two of which were produced in California and two in Germany. You may wish to listen to the stereo mixes to help decide which of the multitracks you want to download first and then jump to the corresponding section for more information on the song and suggestions for things you might try. Two of the songs were distributed as demos inside Studio One. After launching the program and clicking on Demos and Tutorials on the right side of the Start window, you can select "Like the Rain" or "Chill Mode."

AUDIO EXAMPLE 10-1. Louretta: "Like the Rain."

AUDIO EXAMPLE 10-2. Jeffrey A. Fletcher: "Plazma."

AUDIO EXAMPLE 10-3. J&P Project: "Chill Mode."

AUDIO EXAMPLE 10-4. Scott Eric Olivier: "Eavesdrop."

Electronic Music and Studio One

Studio One's free version includes its sample-playing Presence virtual synthesizer, and the paid versions add three more—SampleOne (a sampler), Impact (percussion), and Mojito (subtractive synthesis). These software synthesizers can be placed on Instrument tracks and played by MIDI keyboards.

An in-depth discussion of MIDI, virtual synthesizers, and electronic music production is beyond the scope of this book, but some basic techniques are demonstrated in the videos included with this chapter. Check out the suggested reading at the end of this chapter and the book's companion website if you want more information on Studio One's built-in virtual synthesizers.

CHAPTER AT A GLANCE

Songs.................................123
and Studio One 123
"Eavesdrop"..........................124
"Plazma" 124
Louretta: "Like the Rain" 124
"Chill Mode" 125
For Further Exploration 125

Scott Eric Olivier: "Eavesdrop"

Scott Eric Olivier (casadistortion.wordpress.com) is a producer, engineer, multi-instrumentalist, composer, and pioneer of digital audio technology who has worked with such recording artists as Michael Jackson, Van Halen, Sting, No Doubt, Chris Cornell, the Offspring, Evanescence, and others. As a studio musician, Scott has performed on hundreds of records, playing drums, guitar, bass, synthesizers, and myriad other instruments. Since 1989, he has recorded more than 2,000 live classical and jazz ensembles, engineered 200-plus albums, and played a role on more than 11 million records sold in the United States. He lives in Los Angeles, has worked in 64 countries so far, and his contributions to music, film, and television productions have been enjoyed by millions of people worldwide. He has long been aware of the opportunities and needs of traveling musicians and founded Laptop Roadie in 2005, a first-of-its-kind SFTP SaaS cloud storage system designed for music with group sharing and permissions, which predated other services such as Dropbox, iCloud, and Gobbler.

"Eavesdrop" was composed and performed on a mobile laptop rig while Scott was on the road with the Goo Goo Dolls, and recorded and mixed at Casa Distortion in Los Angeles. The individual blocks of sound were created in Ableton Live and then exported and laid out in Studio One. Video Example 10-1 demonstrates how you can use editing tools to rearrange the sections.

VIDEO EXAMPLE 10-1. Rearranging the blocks with editing tools.

Jeffrey A. Fletcher: "Plazma"

Jeffrey Fletcher (outsourcemusic.us) was an avid Acid Pro user until he became dissatisfied with the performance of certain virtual instruments and the frequency with which the program would crash if he added too many tracks. He began using Studio One and discovered it had a well-organized user interface that didn't have a steep learning curve, that it was efficient to use, and that the Producer and Professional versions allowed him to keep using his favorite third-party VST instruments like Rob Papen's Albino and Camel Audio's Alchemy. He found that the environment was inspiring and made it easier to create more music than before.

Jeff got motivated to create drum-and-bass music after hearing film music and records from Rupert Parkes (a.k.a. Photek). "Plazma," the song featured here, appeared on Jeff's solo EP, released on the label Propa Talent, run by Charissa Saverio (better known as DJ Rap, at djrap.com). Jeff lives in the Los Angeles area, where he produces music for TV (CBS, MTV, Discovery, and the National Geographic channels) and DJs to showcase his drum-and-bass music.

Notice how the Pro EQ on the Drum Bus has been automated, so that the cut-off frequency on the high-pass filter opens up at the beginning of the song and closes back down at the end. Insert a Beat Delay on the Plazma Snare and automate it, as shown in Video Example 10-2.

VIDEO EXAMPLE 10-2. How to create automation to control the level of a delay plug-in.

Louretta: "Like the Rain"

Louretta (louretta.de) lives in Düsseldorf, where she has been creating elektro-rock since 2011. "Like the Rain" was composed and produced by Louretta and Ari Ahrendt on a weekend trip to Hamburg.

Fourteen of the tracks were played on virtual synthesizers—12 with the Presence module, one with Mojito, and one with Impact. Solo each one and start playback from a point in the song at which that instrument is played. Video Example 10-3 shows the type of experiments you might like to try to explore the parameters in PreSonus's Presence virtual synthesizer.

VIDEO EXAMPLE 10-3. Adjusting the parameters of the Presence virtual synthesizer.

The J&B Project: "Chill Mode"

The J&B Project (facebook.com/jbtrance) is a partnership between producers Björn Grashorn and Jan Drapala, and they cite "Chill Mode," a composition by Jan, as an example of the progressive trance music they produce in Hamburg, Germany.

They always start with a kick drum and bass lines and then add a short loop, basic drums, and more percussion. Over this, they layer groove and effects parts and finally a melody. Some of these elements are synthesized with PreSonus's Presence, Access Music's Virus, and Lennar Digital's Sylenth 1 plug-ins. This gives them a four-bar piece of material from which they can extract pieces to build up an arrangement, to which new material is overdubbed.

When you're mixing this song, you might build the elements up in the same order they used to create it, starting with the kick drums and bass and ending with the melody. If you want to remix it and make a new arrangement, you can follow their same method of starting with an intro, establishing a groove, introducing a break, and finding an ending.

FOR FURTHER EXPLORATION

- Read the chapter in the *Studio One Reference Manual* on virtual instruments for information on the four types of synthesizers. Read the section in the chapter on recording pertaining to Instrument tracks.

- See the links for Chapter 10 on the book's companion website, lovelythinking.com.

SETTING UP YOUR STUDIO

CHAPTER 11

GOAL AND OBJECTIVES

After reading this chapter, you should know how to set up and use your equipment to get better mixes.

+ Use meters to avoid distortion.
+ Isolate instruments from the acoustics of the room while you are recording.
+ Achieve a more accurate sound by finding a good position for your monitor speakers.

PREREQUISITES

+ Review the sections in Chapter 1 about frequency response, microphone placement, and phase cancellation.

THEORY AND PRACTICE

This short chapter presents some tips about how to get the best sound while recording and what to do to set up your room for mixing.

Metering

Basing your estimation of how loud something is by the volume it produces in the speakers can be misleading, since it can sound really loud just because you have the speakers turned way up. The amount of amplification controlled with the knob on the amplifier for your speakers is independent of what is going on inside the computer; in fact, the speakers could be turned completely off and the software wouldn't know. By the same token, it's possible to mix very high levels while having your speakers turned down, a practice I recommend in order to protect your hearing, which is one of a musician's greatest assets.

One of the best indicators of the level of the mix can be observed in the meters of the Main Out channel. Keep the levels below 0 dB. If you insert a Level Meter plug-in, it will show that even when it looks like your level is not going above 0 dB, there are actually fast transients that go above it. That is OK because the software gives you some *headroom*—additional dynamic range for transients that are hard to catch visually before you actually clip the signal and cause distortion. Studio One will tell you if there are any clipped samples during the exporting process.

Tracking Room Acoustics

The tracking room or studio is the space in which the musicians play in front of microphones. Placing microphones close to the instruments will reduce the amount of room ambience that makes it onto the track. It is also helpful to have sound-absorbent materials on the floor, ceilings, walls, and other objects close to the musicians like music stands, so that indirect reflections of the sound do not combine with the direct sound and create changes in tone as a result of phase cancellation. If you're willing to take on a DIY project, there are many designs on the Internet for making your own sound-absorbent panels by wrapping insulation around a frame.

Control Room Acoustics

In Chapter 3, Ken Scott talks about how critical it is to have accurate monitor speakers. Investing in good speakers and setting them up properly may be the most critical investment in producing good recordings, but is often the last thing people think about when they're starting out, a situation that has been made more prevalent by the increasing use of inexpensive earbuds to listen to music.

Your primary pair of speakers should be as neutral as possible, meaning that they should have a flat frequency response that doesn't exaggerate or cut the amplitude of frequencies across the spectrum. This will give you the most accurate impression of the choices you are making when applying EQ to affect the tone of your mix. You may wish to get headphones and an additional set of inexpensive speakers so that you can test your mixes on a variety of systems. If it sounds good on the cheap speakers, it means you're ready to see how well your mix works in the wild, in a variety of rooms and inside cars.

Do most of your mixing at medium volume and then occasionally test it at lower and higher levels, since the tonal balance will change. The bass and treble frequencies are boosted when you play at higher volume levels. Try listening to your mix in different positions in the room, including the doorway.

One tried-and-true technique is to place your speakers in an equilateral position with your head at one point in the triangle. The speakers should be placed symmetrically in the room, ideally firing down the long axis of smaller rooms. Avoid corners and getting too close to the wall in order to avoid bass buildup and phantom images. Aim both speakers at your head. The high frequencies should be coming straight at your ears to be heard the best. Put the speakers on absorbing material or on stands so that your table doesn't become part of the acoustic system, and reduce the reflectivity of your table. Have someone walk around the perimeter of your room with a hand mirror. Consider treating the area around the positions of the mirror in which you can see the speakers reflected, since that is an area in which the sound will bounce off the walls and interfere with the direct sound traveling from the speakers to your ears, causing the tone to change.

Have a collection of well-produced music that you know well on hand, with examples of the same style of music that you are working on. Compare these gold standards with your EQ and volume balance settings to gain some perspective. Plug in a Spectrum Meter on the Main Out and see if your overall tone is in the right ballpark. If the bass and treble ranges of one of the classics sounds about as loud as your mix, then you can be confident your mix will sound good on a variety of systems.

ACTIVITIES

The following activities are designed to help you become more aware of the effects of your listening space, the type of speakers you are using, and where they are placed in a room. This is something that most people generally don't pay attention to, but it can make a big difference in how things sound, so take your time and observe the changes.

Basic

Listen to the same piece of music on as many sets of loudspeakers and earphones as possible at home and on the go. Take notes on how they have been set up in the room and the brands and models that sound the best to you.

Intermediate

Listen to well-recorded music on speakers in a room. Change your position and the arrangement of the speakers and take notes on any differences you observe. Try optimizing the acoustic environments you may have at home for listening to music and watching TV or playing video games.

Advanced

AUDIO EXAMPLE 11-1. Pink noise.

Listen to some well-recorded music on the speakers in a room. Play the provided recording of pink noise continuously through your system and move around the room, noticing how the changes in sound that you hear are reported by the software. After arranging your speakers and listening position correctly, insert a Pro EQ filter on the Main Out and change the curve of the filter to compensate for any nonlinearity caused by your speakers. Pink noise has equal energy in every octave, so if your speaker response is completely flat, you should see a flat response in your app. Cut any bands that are coming through too high and boost any that are too low so that your spectrum analyzer's readout becomes as flat as possible. Listen to the well-recorded music again and see if it sounds better to you now. If it does, you might consider saving the Pro EQ's settings and using them on other projects to help you make better decisions while you're mixing.

CHAPTER 12

DIGITAL AUDIO

GOAL AND OBJECTIVES

After working through this chapter, you should understand what sample rate and bit depth are and how analog waveforms are converted to samples.

+ Be able to choose an appropriate sample rate and bit depth for a project.
+ Recognize common audio files types (WAV, AIFF, and MP3).

PREREQUISITES

+ You will need to know what frequency is and that it is measured in hertz (Hz) and kilohertz (kHz) (Chapter 2).

THEORY AND PRACTICE

This brief chapter contains the basic information necessary to pick the right sample rate and bit depth for your projects, and to choose a good setting for buffer size when tracking and mixing. Visit the book's companion website to learn how audio waveforms are converted to digital form in a process called *analog-to-digital conversion* (a.k.a. *sampling*).

Sample Rate

The "frame rate" of movies and video refers to the number of pictures the eye is shown in a second to fool it into thinking it is seeing motion. *Sample rate* in audio refers to how many samples are used to represent one second of audio. Notice how the analog wave in Figure 12-1 has been measured at 31 points in one second. The sampler performing these measurements would be said to be operating at 31 samples per second, or 31 Hz.

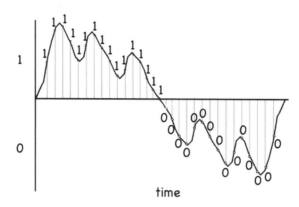

Figure 12-1. A sampler operating at a sample rate of 31 Hz.

The 31 Hz sample rate shown in Figure 12-1 might be suitable for moving images, but is not nearly fast enough for audio. The *Nyquist theorem* (named for Harry Nyquist) states that the sample rate has to be at least twice as high as the highest frequency being recorded. Since humans hear up to around 20 kHz (20,000 cycles per second), CDs were designed to use a sample rate of 44.1 kHz (44,100 samples per second)—a little more than two times 20,000. Stereo CDs store 44,100 samples for each second for the left speaker and another 44,100 for the right speaker. DVDs use a sample rate of 48 kHz.

Bit Depth

Each of the 44,100 samples on a CD are represented as a binary number of 16 binary digits (bits), each bit being a 0 or a 1. The sampler shown in Figure 12-1 is a 1-bit sampler. Each sample contained one bit, which was either a 0 or a 1. CDs use 16-bit samplers. A 16-bit sample has 16 0s and 1s, like the binary number 1011001010011010. The more bits each sample has, the less noise there is in the signal. The engineers that designed the CD format calculated that the noise introduced by a 16-bit sampler would be below the threshold of a listener's perception.

When DVDs were developed about 20 years later, the precision was increased to 24 bits per sample, thereby lowering the noise floor even more. A 24-bit sample looks like the binary number 100101001101010110010101. Of course, the more bits there are, the more storage space they take up. CD-ROMs hold about 737 MB of data. DVDs, which store video as well as audio, have a capacity of more than six times that—4.7 GB for a single-sided disc with a single layer.

Choosing the Right Settings

The spectacular collapse in the price of hard drives and increase in capacity have been a boon to audio engineers, since these developments allow them to record at higher sample rates and bit depths. Match the sample rate and bit depth to the media you intend to use to distribute the music. Use a 44.1 kHz sample rate with 16 bits per sample if you intend to distribute your music on a CD. If you plan to synchronize with video on a DVD, you should use a sample rate of 48 kHz with 24 bits per sample. Blu-ray discs support 96 kHz and 192 kHz sample rates with 24 bits per sample. You may want to record at these higher rates to future-proof your recordings for systems that may be developed, if your audio interface supports them and your system has the necessary space and processor power.

Answer quiz questions 12.1–12.3, found at the end of the chapter.

File Formats

There are three major categories of audio file formats:

1. Uncompressed: such as WAV (PC) and AIFF (Mac OS). These are high-quality versions that require the most amount of storage space and are a good choice for storing and archiving a master recording.

2. Lossless compression: such as FLAC, M4A, and WMA lossless. These use about half the space of uncompressed files by reducing the amount of space used for silences, without losing any quality.

3. Lossy compression: MP3, AAC, WMA lossy. These formats reduce the file size the most by removing and/or simplifying some of the audio information.

We saw in Chapter 2 how the dynamic range of a recording can be reduced by using a compressor plug-in. File compression is something different and has to do with file size. The MP3 file format was the first compressed audio file format to become popular and can be used to encode audio files into bit streams of different sizes and resulting qualities. There is a trade-off between file size and audio quality. The lower the bit rate gets in the compressed file, the more of the original quality of the uncompressed CD will be lost.

Format	Bit Rate	Size per Minute	Quality
wav	uncompressed	10 MB	CD
mp3	160 kbps	1.5 MB	good
mp3	128 kbps	1 MB	fair
mp3	96 kbps	700 KB	poor
mp3	64 kbps	400 KB	bad

Figure 12-2. Comparison of the quality and size of WAV and MP3 files.

Compare the excerpt in Audio Example 12-1 from Sam Broussard's "Times Like These" in the CD's WAV file with the four MP3 files encoded with various bit rates in Audio Examples 12-2 through 12-5. The differences will be more apparent if you have good-quality speakers or headphones and are listening in a quiet environment.

AUDIO EXAMPLE 12-1. Full fidelity WAV file (2.9 MB).

AUDIO EXAMPLE 12-2. MP3 at 160 kbps. The file size is 336 KB.

AUDIO EXAMPLE 12-3. MP3 at 128 kbps. The file size is 269 KB. Notice a drop in the airiness and clarity of the mix, especially the vocal.

AUDIO EXAMPLE 12-4. MP3 at 96 kbps. The file size is 201 KB. Listen to the closed hi-hat and note that it is losing some of its sizzle.

AUDIO EXAMPLE 12-5. MP3 at 64 kbps. The file size is 134 KB and the compression artifacts are now clearly heard.

Latency

Latency is the amount of delay in a system—for example, the amount of time between when you press a keyboard key and when you hear the sound come out. Performers can ignore delays of tens of milliseconds, but when there is a range around a few hundredths of a second, it becomes very distracting or even makes it impossible for them to play. Latency results from the computer using a buffer to temporarily store audio while it performs its calculations. The smaller the buffer, the less latency there will be, but the fewer plug-ins and tracks you can use. Decrease the buffer size while recording if the latency becomes distracting. This may degrade the playback sound or cause clicks, but once you are finished recording, you can switch the buffer back to a larger value while you are mixing to hear the higher-quality sound.

The buffer size is set in Studio One in the Device Block Size field, which you can find under Preferences > Options > Audio Setup. If latency becomes an issue, reduce the buffer size—set it to something like 128 samples temporarily, and then back up to 512 when you are through recording and ready to mix. Some interfaces allow musicians to monitor what they are playing through the interface itself, rather than by looping through Studio One. This is called *zero-latency monitoring* (ZLM). Check your interface to see if it has a mixer control knob to blend the input signal with the signal coming back from the computer. Setting the knob to the input side will emphasize what you are recording and will give you zero latency. Remember, however, to not leave the knob turned all the way to the input side, or you won't hear the music playing back from the computer when you're ready to listen back.

Answer quiz question 12.4.

REVIEW

The takeaways from this chapter are:

+ Your system has to sample at least twice as fast as the highest frequency you want to represent. CDs use a sample rate of 44.1 kHz. Blu-rays can operate at 96 kHz or 192 kHz. If you have enough storage space and a fast enough system, you may wish to record at these higher rates to be able to adapt your material to future systems.

+ Bit depth refers to how many bits each sample is made of. The more bits per sample, the less hiss there is when playing back. CDs have 16 bits per sample. DVDs and Blu-rays have a bit depth of 24 bits.

+ MP3 and other compressed audio file formats shrink the size of files. The lower the bit rate, the more degradation there will be. A data rate of 160 kbps or above is adequate for most listeners and allows them to store more songs on their devices, and the loss of quality is not noticeable when played on lower-fidelity gear like earbuds.

ACTIVITIES

Industry-standard formats make it possible to take files created with one piece of software or hardware and open them with another. Try some of the following activities to apply your new understanding of file formats when moving between different programs like iTunes and Audacity.

Basic

Learn to use iTunes to convert the WAV files you have created in exercises from previous chapters to MP3 format. You can get the free software from Apple's website. See the supplemental material on the book's companion website at lovelythinking.com for more information.

Intermediate

Use a tool like Audacity to convert WAV files to MP3 format. After installing the free software, you will need to download and install the additional LAME MP3 encoder. See the supplemental material on the companion website for more information.

Advanced

Learn about the differences between constant and variable bit rates in MP3 encoding. Experiment with different-quality settings to find those that sound good to you, depending on the type of signal. A lower bit rate can be used for speech and less complex music.

FOR FURTHER EXPLORATION

See the supplemental information on the book's companion website for an introduction to digital audio. Learning more about digital-to-analog conversion and the binary number system used to represent samples will give you a deeper understanding of what sample rate and bit depth refer to.

QUIZ QUESTIONS

12.1: What are the sample rate and bit depth used on compact discs?

12.2: What are the sample rate and bit depth for audio on a DVD?

12.3: What are the sample rate and bit depth for Blu-ray discs?

12.4: If you experience an unpleasant amount of latency while recording a track, should you increase or decrease the buffer size?

Answers to the quiz questions can be found in Appendix C.

APPENDIX A: SUPPLEMENTAL MEDIA

To access the supplemental media, see the instructions that come with your password. The supplemental media include the audio and video examples referenced in the book, along with the Studio One multitrack session files for the mixing exercises.

Visit the book's companion website at lovelythinking.com for updates on the delivery of this material as the system evolves, along with additional information on the content of the chapters, songs, and opportunities to ask questions and share your work.

APPENDIX B: HOW TO INSTALL STUDIO ONE

You can download the Studio One software from the PreSonus website (www.presonus.com/products/studio-one/download). There are four different versions, each with a different number of resources. The demo version of the Professional version will time out after a month. Studio One Free will not time out and is adequate for most of the exercises.

Go to the PreSonus website at www.presonus.com and then click on Technical Support to create a new account. After registering the software you will receive instructions by email with information on how to activate it. If your computer is not connected to the Internet, go to a computer that is connected to the Internet and visit studioone.presonus.com/registration.

The book's companion website (www.lovelythinking.com) has updates about PreSonus's support offerings and obtaining the software.

Once your software is activated you can choose your audio interface by clicking on Studio One > Preferences. You can check to see that you have active inputs and outputs then, by clicking on Song Setup and Audio I/O Setup. More detailed information is available in the Setup section of the *Studio One Reference Manual*.

APPENDIX C: ANSWERS TO QUIZ QUESTIONS

Chapter 1

1.1: An audio interface is needed if you have equipment that you want to use and wish to increase the options to connect audio devices to your computer, or you want higher-quality sound. It is not necessary if your computer has a headphone jack and all you want to do is practice mixing the song session files that come with this book.

1.2: An electric violin should be plugged into the same instrument jack used for an electric guitar or bass. The cable will most likely terminate with a quarter-inch plug.

1.3: Some televisions and audio interfaces have digital connectors. Otherwise, you are most likely to use RCA cables and plug into the line input, if you have one, on your audio interface.

1.4: Most audio interfaces have red LED indicators to temporarily show that the input is peaking. On the screen, a persistent red light comes on.

1.5: Pressing the +48V button on an audio interface or mixer will send phantom power through the microphone cable to the microphone. It doesn't need to be pressed when dynamic microphones are used, since they would make no use of it. The ribbon in some ribbon microphones can be damaged by it. Dynamic and most ribbon microphones can't use phantom power.

1.6: The pad switch cuts the input level and is used when you are recording a very loud source whose level is too high even when you have the preamp turned all the way down.

1.7: Running a quarter-inch cable that far might weaken the signal, and the long wire would be prone to picking up noise. It would be better to connect the guitar to a DI box and then run a long microphone cable to the microphone input of the audio interface. Microphone cables are shielded and are wired in such as way as to reduce the amount of noise that is picked up.

1.8: Check whether the +48V switch is engaged. The condenser microphone will not put out a signal without phantom power.

1.9: Check that the input for the track you are recording on is record-enabled and the track is set to receive from the input your mic is connected to.

1.10: You should see the level in the track's meter. It will work only if you set the track's input to the port that you have the microphone connected to on the audio interface, and arm the track for recording.

1.11: There are many factors that can prevent a signal from being recorded. To systematically catch them all, you may wish to follow the signal path from the top (the sound source) to the end (the loudspeaker playing the sound back). Are they talking? Is the mic close enough to their mouth? Is it plugged in? Is the cable broken? If you're using a condenser mic, is phantom power turned on? If it's a condenser microphone with an internal battery, has the battery pooped out? Which is the input that they are plugged into—the one that the track is set to record from? Is the knob for the preamp for that channel on the audio interface turned up enough? Is the channel you're recording on enabled? The troubleshooting process continues in the next question.

1.12: After you record something, you should see the waveform in the Arrange window. If the line is flat, you're not getting any signal.

1.13: Have you rewound to the start of what you recorded? Have you pressed the space bar or clicked on the right-pointing arrow or pressed the enter key to start playback? You know playback is under way when the cursor is moving across the window and the numbers indicating its location are advancing in the transport bar. It may be that your output settings are not set correctly. Check Studio One > Preferences > Audio Setup and see what device the software is sending the audio to. If it's going to your computer speakers, are they turned on? If it's going to your audio interface, do you have headphones connected to it? Connecting headphones to your computer's headphones jack will not give you any sound if the program is sending the output to your audio interface. Is the volume knob on your interface turned up? Start with your output levels turned down a ways. If you have them turned way up and later correct the setting in the preferences panel, you may end up assaulting your ears with a painfully loud blast. Sometimes it looks like all the output settings are set up correctly in the software, but if you've made some changes while the program is running, you may have to restart the program or even the computer itself for everything to register and work correctly.

1.14: A battery may run out at an inconvenient point during a recording session. Phantom power keeps going as long as you have the button pressed and the interface turned on.

1.15: Dynamic microphones are more rugged, making them more likely to be able to survive being knocked onto the ground.

1.16: The Shure SM57 is a dynamic microphone with a cardioid pickup pattern. It is often used to record snare drums and guitar amplifiers.

1.17: Condenser microphones generally provide a clearer sound.

1.18: Another name for directional is *cardioid*, named for the shape of the pickup pattern. The point in the heart indicates that it records best from one direction (the front). Omnidirectional microphones have a circular pickup pattern, showing that they record with equal strength from all sides.

1.19: Omnidirectional mics are good for recording the overall sound from an instrument like an acoustic bass or piano, or picking up a group of singers or instruments. A cardioid mic is a better choice if you want to avoid feedback or picking up sounds from other nearby sources.

1.20: Sound can travel indirectly to a microphone or listener by bouncing off any reflective surfaces in a room, such as the floor and ceilings, walls, music stands, windows, and pianos.

1.21: The longer the path that the direct sound travels, the softer it gets in proportion to the reflected sound.

1.22: The proximity effect happens when a directional (cardioid) mic is placed close to a sound source, causing a boost in the bass frequencies.

1.23: Singers put out blasts of humid air, pianos don't.

1.24: Space two microphones at least three times as far apart from each other as the closest microphone is to a sound source.

1.25: When signals from two microphones that are picking up the same sound source are combined, the one that is farther away will be delayed and therefore out of sync with the other. When the signal from one is cresting and the other is in a trough, they will cancel each other out. If the mics are spaced far enough apart, the delayed signal will be significantly weaker and will not interfere as much.

Chapter 2

2.1: Engineers use dB (decibel) units to measure the volume of sound.

2.2: A transducer converts energy from one form to another.

2.3: A graph of a waveform shows changes in amplitude (Y axis) over time (X axis).

2.4: Clipping occurs when a signal exceeds the maximum or minimum allowed values. Turn down the preamp gain if you are clipping while recording. Turn down some of the faders on the different tracks (or the fader on the main mix) when you are clipping while mixing.

2.5: The waveform shows three words. A is fairly soft; B is the best because it is a hot signal but does not clip; and C clips toward the beginning, causing distortion.

2.6: Normalizing turns the loudest instant in a track to maximum volume, and increases everything else proportionally to it.

2.7: Normalizing a clipped signal won't do anything, since the level is already at the maximum in the places where it has been clipped.

2.8: Recording automation saves you from having to make the same controller moves every time you listen to a mix. It is also in effect when the song is exported.

2.9: Automation envelopes store the changes in levels that automated controls will go through. They appear underneath the waveform in the Arrange window.

2.10: You can make a song fade out by automating the fader for the Main output.

2.11: The threshold is the level above which the compressor will be activated. The attack time is the length of time the compressor waits before starting to turn the signal down after the input has exceeded the threshold. The release time is the length of time the compressor waits to stop turning the signal down after the input has dropped back down below the threshold. The ratio indicates how strong the compression is.

2.12: Compressors reduce the dynamic range by turning down signals that go above their threshold. Afterward, there is less variation between the softest and loudest sounds.

2.13: Classical recordings are not usually compressed because the composers (e.g., Mozart, Beethoven, Brahms, Ellington) indicated in their scores the dynamics they wished to have the performers play and the listening experience benefits from a big dynamic range. Find an opportunity to attend a wind ensemble or symphony orchestra concert and pay attention to the variations in volume (and tone). Heavy metal is much more consistently loud, and engineers often compress individual tracks as well as the entire mix to raise the level as much as possible. Figure 2-18 shows an overview of the fourth movement of Beethoven's Ninth Symphony. Notice the frequent changes in dynamics and variations between soft and loud. Figure 2-19 shows an overview of "Peace Sells" by Megadeth. Notice how almost the whole mix is at maximum volume, no doubt aided by the use of audio compression.

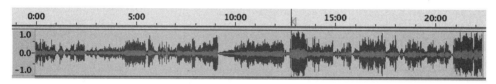

Figure 2-18. Beethoven's Ninth Symphony (IV).

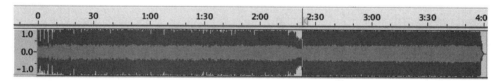

Figure 2-19. Megadeth's "Peace Sells."

2.14: Turning up a compressed track is less likely to cause distortion because its loudest parts have already been turned down before the whole track is boosted. If you turned up the same track without compressing it first, the boosted peaks might clip.

2.15: Tremolo is a modulation of volume. Vibrato is a modulation of pitch.

2.16: Acoustics is the study of mechanical waves in gases and solids. We are interested in what it tells about how pressure waves behave in closed spaces. Psychoacoustics is a field of study combining psychology with acoustics, from which we can learn about how the human brain interprets the electrical signals generated by the inner ear in response to pressure waves.

2.17: The vibrating string causes variations in air pressure that are propagated through a space in pressure waves. The pressure wave enters a listener's ear canal, which passes the vibrations to the fluid in the inner ear, where the hairlike stereocilia cells on the organ of Corti vibrate, causing the generation of electrical signals, which are sent to the brain through the auditory nerve.

2.18: The amplitude of a pressure wave is the amount of change (positive or negative) in atmospheric pressure. On a graph, the amplitude is how high or low the waveform goes above or below the line of the horizontal axis. Increasing the amplitude of the signal makes it sound louder. The volume control on a stereo or TV changes the amplitude of the sound it will send out.

2.19: A transducer converts energy from one form to another. A flashlight converts energy from a battery into light. The pickups on a guitar convert the vibrations of the metal strings into an electrical signal. An internal combustion engine converts gasoline into power to turn a car's wheels. The human eye converts light into an electrical signal that travels through the optic nerve to the brain.

2.20: The unit for measuring amplitude or volume is dB. Musicians generally use the words *volume* and *loudness* interchangeably. The word for loudness has a different meaning in psychoacoustics and takes into account the subjectiveness of how volume is perceived by the brain.

2.21: If you have two tracks with the same recording, and one is assigned to the left channel and the other to the right channel, you can make the sound seem to come out of different positions by adjusting the volume fader for each speaker. To make the sound come out of only the left speaker, turn up the fader for the left channel all the way, and turn the fader for the right channel all the way down. To make the sound come out from the middle, you'd turn the faders for both channels up by the same amount. To make it come out between the center and the right speaker, you'd turn the right fader up more than the left one.

Chapter 3

3.1: In additive mixing, you basically start with everything turned down and gradually turn up the other tracks according to their importance. In subtractive mixing, you start with them all turned up and then turn down the less important ones.

3.2: The piano is barely audible. The electric guitar fills are not much louder than the pedal steel fills, but they are doubled and played a little more confidently so they stand out more. The guitar solo is a little louder than the fills.

3.3: The background singers come in only at some very specific spots and are not as loud as the lead singer, so they blend well and don't stick out.

3.4: The fills are about the same volume in both songs, but the single acoustic guitar in "Sacred Ground" is louder than the doubled ones in "Easy Street."

3.5: During the verses ("All I ever wanted . . . so the dream was planted"), the rhythm guitars are fairly loud but quite sparse. The thin texture lets her voice come through even though Magda is singing in her lower register. During the choruses ("I can't live this way here without you"), the guitars sustain the chords more and blend with an organ pad. The background, even though it is thicker here, doesn't cover up the vocal since the singer is in her higher, more brilliant range and the guitars have been turned down.

3.6: The doubled lead vocal track comes in at the end of second verse on the refrain line ("I'm down, I'm on the ground").

3.7: The background groups sing "on Easy Street . . . I'm down, I'm on the ground" This adds emphasis to the most important lyrics of the song—the refrain and the title line of the song.

3.8: The low background singers first appear in the third verse (V3) and sing the title line ("on Easy Street") once.

3.9: All the tracks will have reverb applied if the effect is inserted into the main mix.

3.10: Audio Example 3-21 has a softer guitar part than Audio Example 3-20.

3.11: The guitar part in Audio Example 3-22 is not as sustained and is louder than the guitar part in Audio Example 3-21.

3.12: Audio Example 3-23 has the guitar coming out of only the left channel, whereas Audio Example 3-22 has the guitar in the center.

3.13: In Audio Example 3-24 the guitar part is doubled throughout, as is the voice on the refrain ("A long way from home").

Chapter 4

4.1: When the box next to Snap is checked, snapping mode is on.

4.2: Snapping mode is useful when you want to edit music that was recorded to a click track and you have the right quantize value set for the grid.

4.3: It is difficult to edit material that was not recorded with a click with snapping turned on, because selections will snap to the grid, which has no relationship to the timing of the recording.

4.4: The note value chosen for quantization determines the spacing of the grid lines.

4.5: Punching in and out automatically engages recording over a specified section in an existing recording. It allows the engineer to precisely set up the region to be recorded.

4.6: When punching in, the recording will take place between the in and out points, which are set by dragging across the bar above the time ruler.

4.7: Studio One uses Preroll to stand for a recording function. When Preroll is on and you start recording, the program will back up and start playback from a position a specified number of bars before, will begin when it reaches the spot you set to start recording, and then will continue until you stop the recording.

4.8: Three elements are needed: new recordings for the introduction and the ending and the previously edited material. The three audio events can be dragged into order on a track. The transition between events can be smoothed by selecting the two regions and creating a crossfade (shortcut x) and adjusting their boundaries if necessary.

4.9: You can create a rhythm track more quickly from a selection consisting of a number of full bars using the Duplicate command (shortcut d), since it creates a string of copies back to back. If you want to make a copy of an audio event and have a gap between the original and the copy, it would be easier to copy it and then paste it where you want it to go.

4.10: Snapping and quantizing work only when the beat in the music agrees with the bars as defined by the program. When the metronome is turned on while recording, the click is the computer's indication of where the beats are.

4.11: Using the tools presented in this chapter, the best way to adjust the timing of hand claps with a track that wasn't recorded with a click would be to isolate each clap and drag/nudge them into place by hand. If you plan to record often without a click, you will want to learn about tempo mapping, so that you can conform a recording to a metronome after the fact and quantize events automatically.

4.12: Transients are short, high-frequency vibrations that signal the beginnings of notes.

4.13: Transients can be found in the initial attack of many instruments, such as a struck percussion instrument, plucked string, or consonant sound in speech.

4.14: Transients usually happen at the start of a note and have a higher amplitude than the surrounding sounds. Editing software finds them easy to locate and mark, saving the user from having to search for them.

Chapter 5

5.1: Tone 1 is spectrum A, Tone 2 is spectrum C, and Tone 3 is spectrum B.

5.2: The spectrum shows the amplitude (vertical axis) and frequency (horizontal axis) of sine waves that make up a sound.

5.3: A waveform shows how the amplitude (vertical axis) of a signal changes over time (horizontal axis).

5.4: A spectrum shows the tone of the sound, which could be helpful when considering changes in EQ settings.

5.5: When editing, it helps to see the starts and ends of words or notes and to find quiet places where edits can be made that won't be obvious to the listener.

5.6: A low-pass filter reduces the amplitude of frequencies above the cut-off frequency.

5.7: A high-pass filter reduces the amplitude of frequencies below the cut-off frequency.

5.8: A band-pass boosts or cuts frequencies around a center frequency.

5.9: Audio Example 5-22 was boosted in frequency band 3; 5-23 was boosted in band 1; and 5-24 was boosted in band 2.

5.10: Audio Example 5-26 was boosted in frequency band 1; 5-27 was boosted in band 2; 5-28 was boosted in band 4; 5-29 was boosted in band 3.

5.11: Audio Example 5-30 has more energy around 700 Hz than Audio Example 5-31.

Chapter 6

6.1: MixVerb is the simplest of the two reverb plug-ins to use and requires less of the computer's processing power.

6.2: Increasing the Size setting makes the reverb last longer.

6.3: The Mix knob controls the wet/dry balance. The wetter the sound is, the more reverb there is in the signal. One way to set the balance is to turn up the reverb until you can hear it clearly and then back off a little to create a subtler effect.

6.4: The volume of the room mic determines the wet level.

6.5: Instruments on tracks with reverb generally sound more distant than those without it.

6.6: Adding reverb to the Main Out adds the same ambience to the entire mix. This can make all the instruments seem as if they were recorded in the same space.

6.7: You may get a cleaner mix if some instruments, like the bass, are not reverbed. In this case, you would add reverb only to the instruments that benefit from it, like vocals, which can then have a longer reverb tail if desired than what you would normally apply to the drums.

6.8: A binaural recording system captures the effects caused by the listener's head and ears on the timing, tone, and amplitude. Playing these back right at the opening of the ears re-creates the conditions under which they were recorded. When the same tracks are played back through loudspeakers, the acoustics of the room and the listener's position relative to the speakers interfere with the effect.

6.9: Echo is a delayed sound that is perceived as a distinct event. Reverberation is a mass of delayed sounds that are not individually perceived, but rather create the impression of space.

6.10: Ambience is the feeling of being in a particular space. Direct sound is the part of the sound wave that reaches the listener's ears in a direct line from the sound source. Reflected sound comes indirectly from the source after bouncing off objects in the environment.

6.11: Reverb plug-ins offer a balance control so you can decide how much processed and unprocessed sound you want to hear. In EQ, you usually just want to hear what the effect is—you set the amount of effect in each frequency band by changing the shape of the curve in the filter's frequency response.

Chapter 12

12.1: CDs have a sample rate of 44.1 kHz and bit depth of 16 bits.

12.2: DVDs have a sample rate of 48 kHz and bit depth of 24 bits.

12.3: Blu-ray discs have a sample rate of 96 kHz or 192 kHz and a bit depth of 24 bits.

12.4: Decreasing the buffer size will reduce the amount of latency. You may also be able to solve the problem by turning the mix knob on your audio interface more toward the input side.

GLOSSARY

3:1 rule. Placing microphones at least three times as far apart as they are from a sound source helps reduce phase cancellation.

Accurate. A musician is accurate when playing a part correctly. A microphone or loudspeaker is accurate if it has a flat frequency response and is not cutting or boosting a particular frequency band.

Acoustics. The study of sound and how it moves through space.

Ambience (or ambiance). Background noise or reverberation that is added to a recording to create the impression that it was recorded live in a particular place.

Amplitude. The amount of positive or negative change in atmospheric pressure as a sound wave travels through the air.

Analog-to-digital conversion (a.k.a. sampling). The process of converting analog audio signals into a series of binary numbers suitable for computer processing. The reverse process (digital-to-analog conversion) takes the binary signal used by computers and turns it into an analog signal that can then drive the drivers in loudspeakers or earphones.

Attenuate. Reduction in amplitude. An *attenuator* is a control that turns the level of a signal down.

Audio interface. Converts microphone and instrument signals to and from digital format. Example: PreSonus AudioBox.

Auxiliary track. Audio tracks write samples to the storage media and read them back. Auxiliary tracks process the signals coming from audio tracks, usually with the plug-ins inserted on them.

Band-pass filter. Trims away frequencies below or above a specified band.

Binaural recording. Intended for playback with earphones, so that each of the two channels of the recording is heard by only one ear. Allows the most controlled environment for creating vivid spatial listening experiences.

Boost. Turn up. Make a particular range of frequencies louder.

Buffer size. The size of the memory that is temporarily holding the signal while it is being processed. Larger buffers give the computer more time to do the mathematical calculations needed to process signals. The bigger the buffer, the more the computer can do for you, but the longer it takes to do it, adding latency—a delay that can interfere with playing new parts in sync with previously recorded tracks.

Bumper. Music put at the beginning and/or end of a program to provide an atmosphere for listening.

Bus. A path that audio can go through in a mixer other than the left and right main channels.

Center frequency. The frequency in the center of a specified band of frequencies.

Chorus. An effect caused by a mix of sounds of roughly the same pitch and tone, such as a section of violins in the orchestra or a group of singers. It is produced electronically by mixing the direct sound with one or more delayed copies of itself that are pitch-modulated with a low-frequency oscillator (LFO).

Clip. The amplitude of a signal cannot go above the maximum allowed or below the minimum. When the limits are reached, the waveform at that point becomes flattened at the extremes, potentially causing audible distortion.

Close miking. Recording from a few inches away.

Comping. Can mean giving someone a free ticket to a show, or improvising an accompaniment in response to what a jazz soloist is playing. In the context of audio production, we mean the process of assembling a track by recording the best sections from several tracks to create a composite track.

Component. An individual sine wave that is part of a more complex sound.

Compression. Three meanings, depending on the context:

Acoustics: areas in space where air molecules are pressed together.
Audio: automatic volume control to smooth out changes in amplitude.
Data: reducing the size of audio files—e.g., in MP3 files.

Cut. Turn down. Make the frequencies in a particular range softer.

Dead air. In broadcasting, this refers to an unintended interruption of silence. In music production, it is a completely silent audio stream.

Decay time. The amount of time it takes for reverb to drop by 60 dB.

Digital Audio Workstation (DAW). A computer with an audio interface and recording software.

Direct sound. The sound that reaches the listener's ears straight from the vibrating object without any reflections.

Double tracking. The process of recording a second track that closely matches the first track. The inevitable slight variations of pitch, tone, and timing between the two tracks create a fatter sound. Doubling can also be done automatically by combining a track with a slightly delayed version of itself.

Dynamic range. The amount of difference between the softest and loudest sounds in a piece. Classical music and jazz usually have a larger dynamic range than heavy metal, even though the latter is likely to be louder overall.

Echo. A repetition of sound that is delayed long enough to be perceived as a separate audio event. A *slapback* echo is approximately 40–120 ms and sometimes used to draw attention to electric guitar or vocal tracks. Slapback simulates the reflection off the opposing wall in a room, usually the longest dimension. In a small room about 20 feet long, the slapback would be about 40 ms. In a large venue 200 feet long, it would be 400 ms. The slapback, acoustically, gives the brain a cue about the size of the space. It can be used to give the listener a feeling of being in a large space (200–400 ms) before adding any reverb and cluttering up the mix.

Electric instruments. Instruments with vibrating bodies that have pickups to sense vibrations, which are then amplified and eventually heard through loudspeakers or headphones. Examples: electric guitar, electric bass, electric violin.

Electronic instruments. Instruments without vibrating bodies that use electronic circuitry to generate a signal that can be amplified and heard through loudspeakers or headphones.

Equalizer (EQ). Another term for *filter*, used to boost or cut particular ranges of frequencies.

Fader. A slider on a mixer that controls the overall volume of a track.

Feedback. Feedback is heard in a public address system when the output of a loudspeaker is picked up from a microphone and re-amplified, causing a high-frequency squeal. In a delay plug-in, it can be a good thing. In this case, the feedback knob controls how much of the delayed signal is fed back into the delay to be delayed again.

Fill. When players (typically in the rhythm section) fill gaps in lead lines by playing busier, louder, and/or more melodic parts.

Filter. Filters let some things pass while blocking others. In music production, filters are electronic circuits or computer processes that modify the tone of the signals that pass through them.

Fundamental frequency. The lowest-frequency component in a sound. When the spectrum is harmonic, all the components fuse and are perceived by the listener as a single pitch with a particular tone.

FX Channel. A term unique to Studio One. Many programs insert plug-in effects inline on audio tracks. FX Channels sit to the right of audio tracks, making it easy to open and close sets of processes.

Global effects. Effects that affect the entire mix, inserted on the Main Out channel.

Graphic EQ. A type of filter with a large number of faders, each controlling a small band of frequencies. Were the positions of the faders connected with a line, it would look like the frequency response of a single filter.

Hard right, hard left. Tracks panned all the way to the right or left, respectively.

Harmonic. A spectrum made of components that are all integer multiples of the fundamental frequency.

High-pass filter. Lets frequencies above the cut-off frequency pass.

Inharmonic. A spectrum made of components that are not all integer multiples of the fundamental frequency.

Intensity. Sound power.

Latency. The amount of time between what you are doing and what you hear. Reducing the buffer or block size in preference settings causes less delay in the audio signal, but reduces the number of tracks and plug-ins you can use.

LFO. Low-frequency oscillator. A synthesizer oscillator outputs a changing voltage as the building blocks of electronic music, usually within the frequency range of human hearing, from 20 Hz to 20 kHz. Low-frequency oscillators generally oscillate more slowly, below the audible range between 3 and 15 Hz, and are used to modulate other signals. For example, an LFO can create a vibrato effect, or vary the delay time in an echo or chorus plug-in. Antonym for UFO, or Unidentified Flying Object. These are more commonly spotted during live outdoor events than inside recording studios.

Limiter. A compressor with a ratio of 10:1 or more. The threshold becomes a hard limit that the output will not exceed.

Localize. The process of the listener recognizing the location of a sound source.

MIDI. Musical Instrument Digital Interface. A protocol released around 1983 that can be used to pass control signals between computers and instruments.

Monophonic (mono). The same sound coming from one or more loudspeakers.

Mute. Turns the sound of a track off. The mute button on a mixer is usually labeled with an M and turns red when it is in effect. The opposite of mute is *solo*.

Nondestructive editing. Editing a roll of analog tape requires cutting it and reassembling the pieces. In nondestructive editing, the samples are read from storage and reused as many times as desired. Mistakes can be fixed and minds easily changed without losing any of the original material.

Nonlinear storage. Storage that allows nearly instantaneous access to any location in data without having to play through the part leading up to it. A record player is nonlinear because you can play from any spot by dropping the needle onto that spot on the surface of the disc. Analog tape, on the other hand, is not, because it has to be rewound or fast-forwarded to get to a desired spot before playback can begin.

Overdub. Recording a new track while listening to previously recorded tracks.

Overtone. A harmonic or inharmonic component above the fundamental frequency.

Peak. A place in the graph of a waveform where amplitude is highest.

Phase cancellation. The electronic combination of two identical waveforms, but with the second waveform 180 degrees out of phase with the first. The result is silence.

Phase combination. The result of mixing signals from multiple microphones that are positioned close enough to pick up sound from the same instrument. Each microphone receives the sound at a different point in the phase cycle and with a different amount of acoustical reflection. The combination of these acoustical sounds changes the tone of the source.

Plug-in. Software that can be inserted into a track to perform a specific signal-processing operation such as equalization, compression, or reverberation.

Proximity effect. A boosting of bass frequencies produced when recording with a directional microphone placed within a few inches of the sound source.

Punch in/out. The process of automatically starting a recording at one preset place in a song and stopping in another.

Q. The slope or resonance of a filter. Greater values create a steeper slope in a filter's frequency response, and a bump around the cut-off frequency where frequencies are boosted.

Quantize. Quantization in time moves events to the nearest beat subdivision of the time grid.

Reference mixes. Favorite, well-recorded music that is played in a studio alongside the current project to provide some perspective.

Reflected sound. The part of a sound that is not *direct sound*. When a pressure wave reaches a wall, floor, or ceiling, it bounces off the surface and eventually reaches the listener's ears after having traveled an additional distance.

Resonance. The ringing of certain frequencies, depending on the dimensions of the space in which they are heard. This effect can be quite noticeable in tiled bathrooms, where certain pitches are amplified.

Reverberation (reverb). The sustain of a sound in a room caused by the continued reflections off all of its surfaces until the sound eventually dies away.

Room mic. A microphone set back in the room to capture the natural reverberation of the space, usually mixed in with microphones placed closer to the instruments.

Room noise. The ambient noise in a room without anyone intentionally making additional sounds.

Session. A recording session is a period of time during which a sound recording is made. In this book, a *song session* refers to a multitrack recording in Studio One format, which is a combination of a .song file and the audio files that each track plays.

Signal path or signal flow. The route that audio signals go through, including the internal path inside pieces of equipment as well as the connections between devices.

Slope. The angle of a filter's roll-off.

Solo. In a musical performance, a solo is a part played by one person that is intended to be the focus of listeners' attention. On a mixing console, when a track's solo button is engaged, any other track that is not also soloed is turned off. Solo is the opposite of mute.

Spectrum (pl. spectra). A graph of the amplitude and frequency of the sine wave components that go into making a complex sound.

Stereo pair. Two microphones, usually of the same type, set up to capture a stereo recording.

Stereophonic (stereo). Sound coming from two speakers or earphones.

Submix. A mix of a group of tracks within a multitrack session that can then be treated as one element of the entire mix. Drums, horns, and background vocals are examples of tracks that might lend themselves to being combined in submixes, which then reduce the number of elements the engineer must consider when making adjustments.

Synthesizer. A type of electronic instrument. It may have a built-in keyboard or just the electronics in a box without a keyboard, in which case it is called a "synthesizer module."

Take. One of a number of recordings of the same material. Often, takes are numbered to make it easier to identify each one when they are played back.

Texture. A description of the overall quality of a piece of music created by a combination of melody, rhythm, and harmony. The process of mixing can affect the texture of a composition by affecting the thickness and prominence of the various tracks. In popular music today there are often multiple parts—a melody that stands out and others that form a background accompaniment.

Threshold. The amplitude level above which compression is activated.

Time grid. The dividing of time into subdivisions that can be displayed on the computer screen as a series of vertical lines or tick marks. The number of subdivisions of the beat is defined by the quantization unit. Events that are selected and then quantized will be automatically moved toward the nearest subdivision.

Track. "Track" has two meanings. When someone says, "The band released a hot new track," they are referring to the recording of a song they like. In the multitrack recording studio, a track is one layer of a multitrack recording. On a mixing board, each microphone is typically routed into an individual track so that the sound of each instrument can be separately controlled during mixdown.

Transients. High-frequency noise components typically found at the start of a note, especially when played on a percussion instrument.

Tremolo. Cyclical amplitude modulation. The X-Trem plug-in in Studio One provides varying depth and rate of tremolo.

Vamp. A section of a song that is played over and over, sometimes to open up an arrangement and leave a space for an improvisation, or at the end of a song under a fade-out.

Vibrato. Periodic fluctuations in the frequency of a note, most prominently associated with the wobbling pitch of opera singers.

Volume. The intensity of audible sound measured on a logarithmic scale using units of decibels (dB).

Wet/dry balance. Often expressed as a percentage of processed to unprocessed signal. For example, if the wet/dry balance of a reverb plug-in is set to 20 percent, it means that 20 percent of what comes out has been reverberated (is wet), and the rest is unprocessed (dry).

Zero crossing. A point at which the waveform crosses the horizontal 0 amplitude line. Combining two regions at zero crosses eliminates clicks. Many times it is faster just to apply a crossfade after editing two regions that don't meet at 0.

BIBLIOGRAPHY

The purpose of *Getting Started with Music Production* is to help you use computer-based recording software to produce music as quickly as possible. Some basic theory was included to help you understand what is going on and to make effective use of the tools. You may enjoy exploring some of the following books to get different perspective on the material and to learn about more advanced topics.

Dittmar, Timothy A. *Audio Engineering 101: A Beginner's Guide to Music Production*. Burlington, MA: Focal Press, 2012. A well-written companion for *Getting Started with Music Production*, covering topics including people skills, a microphone guide, signal processors, studio session procedures, the history of audio, and job considerations.

Edstrom, William, Jr. *Studio One for Engineers and Producers*. Montclair, NJ: Hal Leonard Books, 2013. Edstrom wrote this book for engineers who already use another program for audio recording and are switching to Studio One. It presents advanced features not covered in this book, such as Audio Bend, Melodyne, groove quantizing, and mastering.

Emerick, Geoff, and Howard Massey. *Here, There, and Everywhere*. New York: Gotham Books, 2006. Emerick describes his involvement with *Revolver*, *Sgt. Pepper's*, and other albums, recording techniques, and the Beatles' process.

Gibson, Bill. *Hal Leonard Recording Method* in six volumes. *Book One: Microphones & Mixers*. *Book Two: Instrument & Vocal Recording*. *Book Three: Recording Software & Plug-Ins*. *Book Four: Sequencing Samples & Loops*. *Book Five: Engineering and Producing*. Available individually or as a box set. An ambitious compendium of all facets of music production, with accompanying discs of audio and video demonstrations.

Huber, David Miles, and Robert Runstein. *Modern Recording Techniques*, eighth edition. Burlington, MA: Taylor & Francis, 2014. A standard survey that contains information on MIDI protocol, multimedia and the Web, synchronization, amplifiers, surround sound, and product manufacturing.

Izhaki, Roey. *Mixing Audio: Concepts, Practices and Tools*. Waltham, MA: Focal Press, 2012. Covers the entire range of mixing and how it affects music.

Major, Mike. *Recording Drums: The Complete Guide*. Boston: Course Technology, 2014. A full 400 pages on recording and mixing percussion.

Oppenheimer, Larry. *Power Tools for Studio One 2: Master PreSonus' Complete Creation and Production Software, Volumes 1 & 2*. Montclair, NJ: Hal Leonard, 2012. A great follow-up to *Getting Started with Music Production*. Covers the advanced features not included in this book, like Melodyne integration and mastering.

Owsinski, Bobby. *Audio Mixing Boot Camp*. Van Nuys, CA: Alfred, 2002. Practical tips, tricks, and secrets.

PreSonus *Studio One Reference Manual*. Found under the Help menu when using the Studio One software.

Scott, Ken, and Bobby Owsinski. *Abbey Road to Ziggy Stardust: Off the Record with the Beatles, Bowie, Elton and So Much More*. Los Angeles: Alfred Music Publishing, 2012.

Thompson, Daniel. *Understanding Audio: Getting the Most Out of Your Project or Professional Recording Studio*. Boston: Berklee Press, 2005. Intended to fill in the gaps in one's understanding of audio and the recording process, covering sound, acoustics, psychoacoustics, and basic electronics, in addition to the use of the recording studio and how signals pass through the mixing console.

Tough, David. "Shaping Future Audio Engineering Curricula: An Expert Panel's View." *Journal of the Music & Entertainment Industry Educators Association*, vol. 10, no. 1 (2010). Notice the preponderance of personal characteristics that are valued in people working in the industry, such as work ethic, communication skills, and conscientiousness.

INDEX

ABOUT THE AUTHOR

Robert Willey was born in Menlo Park, California, and grew up using two- and four-track tape recorders, listening to new releases from the Beatles, and later performing music from the Baroque and Impressionist periods. He received a bachelor's degree in music from the University of North Texas and, after playing in San Francisco peninsula bands and working at the Hoover Library, attended the University of California, San Diego, where he received a master's degree in computer music and a PhD in theoretical studies. He assisted a music technology exchange program between the Center for Music Experiment (UCSD), the Center for Computer Research in Music and Acoustics (Stanford University), and the Musical Production and Research Laboratory (Buenos Aires, Argentina), funded by the Rockefeller Foundation, and then received a Fulbright Scholarship to teach computer music performance and composition at the Federal University of Minas Gerais in Belo Horizonte, Brazil. He then stayed on for a year to teach arranging, chamber music, improvisation, and piano at the Carlos Gomes Foundation and the Federal University of Pará in Belém, Brazil.

After returning to the United States, Willey taught popular music theory and directed the rock band at the State University of New York at Oneonta, and music production, technology, and music industry at the University of Louisiana at Lafayette, before becoming director of the Music Media Production and Industry program at Ball State University in Muncie, Indiana.

His publications include the method books *Louisiana Creole Fiddle* (Alfred Music Publishing) and *Brazilian Piano* (Hal Leonard Corporation), the DVD *From La La to Zydeco* (Center for Louisiana Studies), music for commercials and theater, educational and multimedia materials, and CDs of original compositions (Aucourant Records) and computer music (*The Book of Names, SBCMII, Intercambio/Exchange*).

Website: rkwilley.com

The Entire Recording Process Explained!

The Hal Leonard Recording Method by Bill Gibson is the first professional multimedia recording method to take readers from the beginning of the signal path to the final master mix.

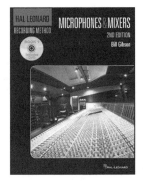

BOOK 1: MICROPHONES & MIXERS – 2ND EDITION
Revised and Updated

Topics include how professional microphones work, which to choose and why (plus accepted techniques for using them), understanding the signal path from mics to mixers and how to operate these critical tools to capture excellent recordings, and explanations of the most up-to-date tools and techniques involved in using dynamics and effects processors.

HL00333253   978-1-4584-0296-7
Book/DVD-ROM/Online Media.........$39.99

BOOK 2: INSTRUMENT & VOCAL RECORDING – 2ND EDITION
Revised and Updated

This edition addresses new equipment and software concerns that affect the way excellent recordings are made. You'll learn what you need to know about capturing the best vocal and instrument tracks possible, no matter what kind of studio you are working in or what kind of equipment is used.

HL00333250   978-1-4584-0292-9
Book/DVD-ROM/Online Media.........$39.99

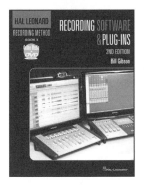

BOOK 3: RECORDING SOFTWARE & PLUG-INS – 2ND EDITION
Revised and Updated

You'll need to know next how recording software programs work and how to choose and optimize your recording system. This book, DVD-ROM, and online media use detailed illustrations and screen shots, plus audio and video examples, to give you a comprehensive understanding of recording software and plug-ins.

HL00333437   978-1-4584-1651-3
Book/DVD-ROM/Online Media........$39.99

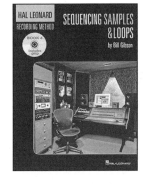

BOOK 4: SEQUENCING SAMPLES & LOOPS

Learn to create amazing music productions using the latest sequencing techniques with samples and pre-recorded loops. With detailed screen shots, illustrations, video and audio examples, and more on the accompanying DVD, you're on your way to rounding out your recording education.

HL00331776   978-1-4234-3051-3
Book/DVD $39.95

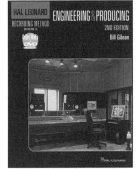

BOOK 5: ENGINEERING AND PRODUCING – 2ND EDITION
Revised and Updated

Learn how to engineer and produce like a pro, recording excellent tracks ready for the mix. This updated edition addresses newer concerns such as social media and making money in today's business climate.

HL00333700   978-1-4584-3692-4
Book/DVD-ROM/Online Media..... $39.99

BOOK 6: MIXING & MASTERING – 2ND EDITION
Revised and Updated

This important second edition demonstrates techniques and procedures that result in a polished mix and powerful master recording, using current plug-ins, software, and hardware. You'll then learn how to prepare the mastered recording for CD replication, streaming, or download. Updated illustrations, photographs, and audio and video examples from the DVD-ROM and online media will reinforce your understanding of what you need to mix and master like the pros.

HL00333254   978-1-4584-0297-4
Book/DVD-ROM/Online Media..... $39.99

HAL•LEONARD®

www.halleonardbooks.com

Prices, content and availability subject to change without notice.

0315